ANCIENT LITTLE KNOWN KNOWLEDGE OF HEALTH AND LONG LIFE.

By

KENYON KLAMONTI

Author of — BREATH AND BLOOD — HEALTH
SCIENCE — SCIENTIFIC LIVING — THE NUTRI-
TIONAL MYTH — LONGEVITY, etc., and the re-
markable course IMMORTALISM.

———

NATURAL SCIENCE SOCIETY
2803 S. Bumby Street
ORLANDO, FLORIDA

"EVOLUTION"
THE MONKEY'S VIEWPOINT

Three monkeys sat in a Cocoanut tree
Discussing things as they're said to be.
Said one to the others, "Now listen you two,
There's a certain rumor that can't be true.
That man descended from our noble race—
The very idea! It's a dire disgrace.
No monkey ever deserted his wife
Starved her baby and ruined her life.
And you've never known a mother monk
To leave her baby with others to bunk,
Or pass them on from one to another
'Til they hardly know who is their mother.
And another thing! You will never see
A monk build a fence 'round a cocoanut tree
And let the cocoanuts go to waste
Forbidding all other monks a taste.
Why if I put a fence around this tree
Starvation would force you to steal from me.
Here's another thing a monk won't do,
Go out at night and get on a stew
Or use a gun or club or knife
To take some other monkey's life.
Yes! man descended, the ornery cuss,
But brother he didn't descend from us!

Author Not Known

FREEDOM OF SPEECH AND OF THE PRESS

We believe in the inalienable and constitutional right of religious liberty, and freedom of speech and of the press as a means of education and conveying God's message to our fellow man, as is guaranteed by the first amendment to the Constitution, which reads:

"Congress shall make no law respecting an established religion, or prohibiting the free exercise thereof; or abridging the freedom of speech or the press; or the right of the people peaceably to assemble, and to petition the government for a redress of grievances."

The five Supreme Court Justices of the State of Florida appeared to be in harmony with this amendment when they showed in a case before them "what is really involved in any attempt to throttle free speech or to choke the press." Concurring in the decision with the others, Judge Chapman rendered a separate opinion, in which he said in part:

"The liberty and freedom of the press under our fundamental law is not confined to newspapers and periodicals, but embraces pamphlets, leaflets, and comprehends every publication which affords a vehicle of information and opinion. The perpetuity of Democracies has as a foundation an informed, educated and intelligent citizenry. An unsubsidized press is essential to and a potent factor in instructive information and education of the people of a democracy and a well-informed people will perpetuate our constitutional liberties."

Quoted in "Liberty," Vol. 37, No. 1, First Quarter 1942, P. 31.

DEDICATION

To all brave men and women who dare face some of life's deepest truths even though they may shatter illusions which people have fondly cherished for ages — and to those who seek a life of super vitality by following natural methods of right living which will bring them a state of physical and mental well being that will usher in a new era of health and happiness on earth.

This volume is dedicated,
by the Author,

KENYON KLAMONTI

"Think truly, and thy thoughts
Shall the world's famine feed,
Speak truly, and each word of thine
Shall be fruitful seed;
Live truly, and thy life shall be
A great and noble creed."

— Horatio Bonar.

ABOUT THE AUTHOR

When the author was a boy and saw children sicken and die under the doctor's care, he lost faith in medicine and began an investigation that he has pursued all his life, and has made some shocking discoveries.

Kenyon Klamonti realized doctors are not interested in NATURE'S METHODS, for these make them unnecessary and damage their business. So they oppose and condemn them in self-defense, as should be expected. He began by putting the LAW of CAUSE and EFFECT into action and searched for CAUSES which is just the reverse of the accepted procedure.

His Health Philosophy is based on God's Eternal Law of Life, which changes not and thus rules out all so-called progress in caring for the sick. There is no progress beyond Truth. What medical art terms progress simply means traveling in a circle.

There is no such thing as "healing." The body repairs itself; and the principal agencies used in the work are pure air, good water, sunshine, exercise and natural food. That is the reason why doctors, drugs, serums and operations always fail.

For years this author tested his Health Philosophy in active practice, and lost not one patient. Practically every one of them was a physical wreck, and came to him only as a last resort, after being cast off by other doctors as hopeless and incurable.

His method is too natural and simple to attract medical art. It is so natural and simple that it appeals to no one because it can be so readily understood and easily applied. Here it is in a few words —

1. The Breath of Life is first (Gen. 2:7). When you stop breathing you stop living. To preserve life the air must be free of pollutants. So he put his patients where they had only fresh, clean air to breathe.

2. The Fluid of Life comes next. Man cannot live long without water. The greater part of the blood and body consist of water. To preserve life the water one drinks must be pure, and free of the pollutants used by political health boards. So he gave his patients only pure rain water to drink.

3. The greatest freedom of Vital Function comes next This is produced by physiological rest of the vital organs, secured only by an absolute fast, giving patients no food but air and water, the two greatest foods of man.

Under this simple, natural regime, his patients recovered as though by magic. The ability of the body to repair itself when given complete freedom to do so is amazing. The author's work proves that so-called disease is an imaginary entity that does not exist. There is Good Health and Bad Health, but no disease. The symptoms of Bad Health the doctors are trained to study, group together and give them names that mean nothing, and term them diseases that must be treated and cured.

That scheme is supported by millions of dollars and centuries of false teaching, by which the doctors have created a false psychology of disease that yields gigantic profits; and woe unto him who interferes with the profitable racket.

PART 1.

ANCIENT LITTLE KNOWN KNOWLEDGE OF HEALTH AND LONG LIFE.

PART 2.

KEY TO VITAL ENERGY.

PART 3.

HEALTH SCIENCE.

Ancient Little Known

Knowledge of Health & Long Life

PART 1.

Ancient records show that ancient people knew secrets of Nature unknown to modern science or modern doctors. They knew how to

(1) promote health, (2) preserve youth, and (3) prolong life.

But a group of men interested only in money and not in the betterment of humanity, are not going to kill the goose that lays the golden egg by learning how to promote health then teach that knowledge to the people. For a world of health would mean the end of doctors and all lines of commercialism that live and thrive on the miseries of man.

The ancient formula of Perpetual Youth was known to the ancients, and they lived nearly a thousand years. But that knowledge apparently was lost with the death of Noah, as evidenced by the fact that after his death the life-span rapidly declines.

Adam lived 930 years (Gen. 5:5), and Noah lived 950 years (Gen. 9:29). From Adam to Noah the life-span averaged 912 years. From Shem, son of Noah, to Nahor, only eight generations, the life-span averaged 354 years. Shem lived 602 years and Nahor 148.

Shem's life-span was 348 years shorter than his father's. That was the first appreciable decline from the days of Adam. In eight generations after Noah the life-span had decreased to 148 years—a startling decline of 802 years in eight generations.

What was the ancient secret that seems to have been lost with the death of Noah?

CONQUER DEATH

The world's history is composed of the issues of Life and Death. The Ancient Masters said:—

> Death is swallowed up in victory (1 Cor. 15: 54). There shall be no more death, neither sorrow, nor crying, neither shall there be any more pain; for the former things are passed away (Rev. 21:4).

Perpetual Youth and Eternal Life have been the dream of philosophers from the dawn of humanity. Down thru the centuries man has searched for the Fountain of Youth and Elixir of Life. Prophets and poets in every age have told of a time when the pain of disease would be unknown, and the sting of death unfelt.

For what is more precious than Life? What is a man profited if he gain the whole world and lose his life?—Mat. 16:26.

Death is the drop of gall in the cup of pleasure. Childhood fears it. Old age dreads it.

Even disease, poverty, crime, shrink from release by it. The beast loves life no less than man.

Consequently, how to promote health, preserve youth and prolong life was the first subject to engage man's serious attention. It is still the leading thought.

The First Scientists

Recent discoveries teach us to have greater respect for Ancient Science. It was the growth of countless ages, and was apparently born in India (Gen. 11:2). The sacred writings of the Hindus give their ancient history an astonishing chronology covering thousands of years (Peerless Atlas, 1903, p. 149).

Modern science is in its infancy. Its career has hardly begun, and its progress is impeded by its materialistic views. It rejects the doctrine of a Supreme Power and a Life Principle. It holds that Life is what it does. Life is *"the expression of a series of chemical changes,"* says Osler, the greatest doctor America ever produced. This leaves the Living World without a law, and leaves science laboring in the dark.

Recently discovered records show the Ancient Masters knew secrets of Nature unknown to us. The fact they lived for centuries is evidence they knew how to preserve the body and prolong its youth. Adam was 130 when he begat his first child, and lived 930 years. Methuselah was 187 when he begat his first child, and lived 969 years (Gen. 5:3, 5, 25, 27).

This vital knowledge seems to have been lost with the death of Noah. He was the last of the Ancient Scientists who appears to have known the secret of the ages. For after his death, the decline in the life-span was very rapid.

As time passed, the decline continued at an alarming rate. In eight generations after Noah, it had dropped from 950 to 148 years—an astounding decline of 802 years!

Behold man's tremendous loss! See his most precious treasure slipping from him. In only eight generations approximately 85 per cent of his life was lost.

Experience teaches that when man saw his life leaving him so fast, his heart was filled with horror. He was being hurried to the grave while yet young in years; and demon death was striking him down ere his work had hardly begun.

The very picture makes one shiver. With the grim monster standing at his door,. slaying many while in the flower of youth, with failure meeting every effort to find ways and means to defeat the demon, the race in desperation turned at last to the idea of a Life Beyond the Grave as the best that could be done.

That was abject surrender. For man is not the victor until he has discovered the Law that makes him master of his destiny, and gives him power to control the conditions that destroy him.

UNIVERSAL LAW

Modern science fails in its work because it rejects the doctrine of a (1) Supreme Power, (2) Life Principle, and (3) Universal Law. On that point Dr. Walter writes:—

"Everything in accordance with law is the testimony of both Science and Revelation; and man becomes the possessor of Earth's treasures as soon as he has discovered the laws of their production. The first real step towards exact knowledge is the discovery of the law. All the investigations, speculations and inductions that man can invent or employ, are worthless until the work is completed by this discovery." (Vital Science, p. 205).

Modern science has incessantly searched for the Fountain of Youth, but has failed in its work because it has not been scientific in its search.

All searchings lead in circles until the fundamental fact is discovered that Man is part of a World of Law and Order. The Supreme Power and the Life Principle are facts of existence, and the Law of Life is as certain as the Law of Gravitation. But medical schools refuse to recognize these things, and continue to grope in darkness.

Every event that takes place, occurs under the control of one law, sustained by one force.

In spite of the fact the medical world denies it, this Principle of Nature applies as forcibly to the human body as to the rising sun.

"No symptoms of health or disease, no pain or pleasure, weakness or strength," writes the shrewd Dr. Walter, "is ever found in a living organism except under the control and direction of the one law, sustained by the one power,—the law that solves all physiological problems." (Vital Science, p. 22).

That statement of Law shows the absurdity of hunting for health in magic waters and mysterious brews, poisonous drugs and filthy serums. It shows that health is not a question of doctors and dope, of vaccines and poisons. It shows why the "practice of medicine" must always be what it has always been—the practice of nonsense, and so declared by leading doctors of the world.

Prof. Majendie, the celebrated French physician, said:

"Medicine is a great humbug. I know it is called science. Science, indeed! It is nothing like science" (Densmore, p. 209).

Dr. Ernest Schwenninger, the famous physician to Prince Bismark, wrote:

"Doctors call medicine 'recognized science.' It is recognized ignorance" (Densmore, p. 207).

What little we know of the operation of the Law of Cause and Effect teaches that, barring accidents, the Health and Duration of the Liv-

ing Body depends upon the conditions supplied.
Dr. Walter states:

> "If we supply the conditions for health, health
> will follow with unerring certainty; but if the condi-
> tions are for disease, disease will sooner or later
> follow as the Law of Adjustment will permit"
> (V.S., p. 122).

That statement agrees with the views of the
Ancient Master who said:

> "Whatsoever a man soweth, that shall he also
> reap." (Gal. 6:7).

It is science and law that we cannot sow
the seeds of disease, and harvest a crop of
health.   Nor can we force into the body such
poisons as medicines, drugs, vaccines and serums, and be favored with good health and long
life.

Let us carry the principle farther if we
supply the conditions of prolonged youth, then
with unerring certainty we shall have prolonged youth.   Also, if we supply the conditions of
long life, then, barring accidents, long life will
follow with unerring certainty.

This appears as the basic principle of the
knowledge lost with the death of Noah Let us
proceed with certainty in a straightforward
manner through infinite time to infinite results

Our next step is to learn how to apply our
new discovery of an old secret.   There is no
use to turn to modern medical lore, for the

bungling work of medical men shows they are wandering in darkness. Their schools teach that health comes from forcing destructive poisons into the body. Centuries of experience proves this is wrong. We must look for a better source. We turn to the teaching of the Ancient Masters who worshipped Truth instead of Mammon.

PATH TO THE GLORIOUS LIFE

Ages of experience show without exception that Simplicity, Frugality and Self-Denial (Mat. 16:24) are the basic qualities that constitute the Path to the Glorious Life.

Listen to the words of Socrates, the sage of centuries ago:

> "Know thyself. Earthly goods advance not their possessor. To want nothing is divine. To want the least possible brings one nearer to divine perfection." (Encyc. Americana, 1938, vol. 25, p. 220).
>
> "The less physical Man becomes through the conquest of his Desire, the less he needs. The less Man needs, the nearer he becomes like gods, who use nothing and are immortal."

The Wise Men of the East (Mat. 2:1) considered Desire a "foul monster," to be conquered by Self Mastery. In the "Message of the Master" we read:

> "As the flame is dimmed by the smoke; and the bright metal by the rust, so is the Understanding of Man obscured by this foe called Desire, which

rageth like a fire, and is difficult of being extinguished. * * *

"Thy first task is to conquer this foul dweller in the Mind. Mastering first the Senses and Sense Organs, do thou then proceed to put to death this thing of evil.

"The Senses are great and powerful. But greater and more powerful than the Senses is the Mind; and greater than the Mind is the Will; and greater than the Will is the Real Self.

"So, thus recognizing the Real Self as higher than all, proceed thou to govern the Personal (Physical) Self. Conquer this foul monster, Desire, most difficult to seize, and yet possible of mastery by the Real Self; then bind him fast forevermore, thy slave instead of thy master." (p. 44).

BODY BUILDING MATERIAL

The Living Body must be furnished constantly with suitable Building Material. This material consists of (1) Air, (2) Water, and (3) Food.

Before the advent of the gas engine, the deadly exhaust of which has poisoned the air of civilization; and—

Before commercialized health boards began polluting the water of civilization with poisonous chemicals, under the pretense of purifying it—

Food was the only element of body-building material to which it was necessary to give particular consideration.

Due to the fact that Excessive Eating is the rule of every animal when food is plentiful, the function of eating is a matter in which the Mind must incessantly exert itself in order to hold Desire in subjection.

While both Air and Water come before and are superior to Food as body-building material, it is not possible to injure the body by the free use of these, provided they are pure and fit for consumption.

The same is not true of Food, unless it is strictly natural, and consists of juicy fruits, such as grapes, apples, oranges, mangoes. peaches, plums, melons, tomatoes, and the water of coconuts.

These are the natural food of man; and aside from these, one must be careful not to eat to excess. For the surplus above the body's needs, not being used, decomposes and ferments in the body, and poisons it.

Sylvester Graham (1794-1851) often said that a drunkard may reach old age, but a glutton, never.

The truth of this assertion is proven by experience. Drakenberg, a Dane, buried in the cathedral in Aarhus, Denmark, lived 146 years—

"And reached this advance age in spite of the fact that he was more often drunk than sober."

writes Dr. Arnold Lorand in his "Old Age Deferred," p. 48.

FRUGAL EATING

Contrary to medical theory that man should eat freely of what doctors call "good, nourishing food," for health and long life, the opposite of this theory is proven in practice to be the Path to the Glorious Life.

A leading case in order is that of Ludovico Cornaro, described in the Ency. Americana as a "Venetian nobleman" (vol. 7, 1938, p. 707). The account states:

> "From the 25th to the 40th year of his age, he was afflicted with a disordered stomach, gout and slow fever, till at length he gave up the use of medicine and accustomed himself to extreme frugality in his diet. * * * In his work upon the 'Birth and Death of Man,' composed a few years before his death, he says of himself:
> "I am now as healthy as any person of 25 years of age. I write daily six or seven hours, and the rest of the time I occupy in walking, conversing, and occasionally in attending concerts. I am happy, * * * my imagination is lively, my memory tenacious, my judgment good, and what is most remarkable in a person of my advanced age, my voice is strong and harmonious."—Ibid.

Of Cornaro, Dr. J. E. Cummins writes:

> "Cornaro (was) the greatest modern food scientist. He was born an invalid and became a drunkard. At the age of 40 he was a physical and mental wreck, and his physicians told him repeatedly that he could not live.
> "Cornaro began to experiment with foods. He found he could live best on 12 ounces of solid food

and 16 ounces of unfermented wine daily. With the exception of 12 days, he lived on this ration for over 63 years. Within one year he had recovered his health. His wife adopted the same course, and bore children late in life.

"Both lived beyond the century mark. On his 78th birthday, Cornaro's friends begged him to increase his ration a little. Reluctantly he agreed to a 14-ounce allowance. In 12 days he was stricken with fever and violent pains in his right side. He at once returned to the 12-ounce ration, but suffered for 35 days.

"This was his only illness in a period of 63 years. Life became more beautiful the older he grew. He wrote several books, his last after the age of 95. He died at the age of 103." (Dietetics).

Cummins holds that man would have better health and longer life if he ate only one-fourth of what he usually consumes. He says:

"In India, at the present time, people eat but one meal a day, and that in the evening. Occasionally they have a little rice water to drink in the morning. They know nothing of digestive troubles.

"In Bible times people ate but one meal a day, and biblical law required that the laborer be paid daily so he could buy his meal. The ancient Persians lived on one meal a day. The Greeks and Romans lived on one or two meals a day. No nation has quite equalled the Greeks in physical perfection." (Dietetics).

K. L. Coe, writing in Correct Eating & Strength, March, 1931, refers to people who live healthy and long, and to the natives of India in particular. He observes:

"Numerous instances of longevity are reported from various quarters, proving that man, under certain circumstances, can live to a much greater age than is customary.

"Perhaps the most striking of these in recent times is furnished by Dr. Robert McCarrison, of the British Army Medical Service in India, who reports that in a colony in the Himalayan region he found natives who were so old that it would be hard to believe their records correct, yet he was not able to detect any error in their way of keeping these records

"Ages well beyond 250 years were common. He found men of well attested age up to 150 years recently married and raising families of children.

"Men said to be well over 200 years of age were working in the fields with younger men, and doing as much work, and looking so much like the younger men, that he was not able to distinguish the old from the young.

"These people were restricted by religious dogma to the products of the soil for food, no animal products being permitted, except a small amount of milk or cheese, which were considered luxuries.

"He reported these people were never sick. They had none of the usual diseases of civilized countries, as they could not afford the expense of the habits which cause these diseases.

"During his nine years in that region, there were no case of indigestion, constipation, appendicitis, etc. In fact, no sickness of any sort. He might as well not have been there, except for the illness and surgery within the army post itself.

"It is possible these people live so long, and are so free from disease, because they live almost entirely on natural foods."

What a lesson civilized man could learn from the simple habits of the people of India and other tropical regions of the earth. But he considers himself so far above these people, that he looks down upon them with disdain.

It has been shown by experiments that great danger lies in excessive eating and in eating artificial and prepared foods.

Dr. Charles W. De Lacy Evans, M. R. C. S. E., etc., surgeon to St. Savior's Hospital, England, and author of several scientific works of unusual interest, wrote an admirable book entitled "How to Prolong Life." In the chapter on "Instances of Longevity in Man and in the Animals and Vegetable Kingdoms," he reviewed nearly 2,000 cases of persons who lived more than a century. After discussing all their various habits and customs, he says:

"We find one great cause that accounts for the majority of cases of longevity—moderation in the quantity of food." (Densmore, p. 295).

Again Dr. Evans writes:

"Among instances of longevity, we have the ancient Britons, whom Plutarch states 'only began to grow old at 210 years.' * * * Their food consisted almost exclusively of acorns, berries and water." (Ibid).

In the February 7, 1878 issue, of the Lancet, a London medical journal, was reported the case of Miguel Solis, of San Salvador, a half-blood Indian, who was then living at the age of 180. The account stated:

"Dr. Hernandez found this man working in his garden. He attributed his long life to his careful habits and eating only once a day. * * * He had been accustomed to fast on the 1st and 15th of every month. He chose the most nourishing foods, and took all things cold." (Densmore, p. 297).

Dr. Arnold Lorand warns against heavy eating. He observes:

"It is certain that more people die from eating too much than too little. It is surprising to consider how little food man can exist upon for a long time and remain in good health; and it is certain that the foundations of many diseases are laid by excessive eating." (Old Age Deferred, p. 280).

VALUE OF FASTING

It is a rule without exception that all animals eat to excess when food is plentiful. Little does modern man know of the damage done to his body by excessive eating.

In the case of the lower animals, experimental tests show the effect of fasting and excessive eating. On this point Prof. C. M. Child, Chicago University, writes:

"Experimental investigations, carried through a number of years in the Department of Zoology of the University of Chicago, have shown these flatworms, when well fed, grow old just as the higher animals do, but that they may be made young again in various ways.

"When these animals are deprived of food, they do not die of starvation in a few days. * * * They are able to live for months upon their own tissues. During the time of fasting they become smaller and may be reduced to a minute fraction of their original size. When fed again after such fasting, they show all the physiological characteristics of young animals. With continued feeding, they go again through the process of growth and of becoming old, and may be made young again by fasting.

"One group of the worms was well fed, and every three or four months passed through the cycle of growing old and reproducing. * * * The other group was given just enough food to maintain the animals at a constant size. The worms of this group remained alive and in good physiological condition without become appreciably older as long as the experiment continued — that is, during some three years.

"With abundant food, this species may pass through its whole life history * * * in three or four weeks. But when growth is prevented by fasting, it may continue active and young for at least three years, as the foregoing experiment has demonstrated, and doubtless for a much longer period.

"According to the observation of Julian Huxley, the extension of the life-span in this experiment is roughly equivalent in man to keeping a person alive from the time of Chaucer (1340-1400) down to the present date."

Fasting and frugal diet kept worms alive for three years that die in three or four weeks when well fed. Had the experiment continued longer, the worm perhaps could have been kept alive longer.

If this could be done with a man who lives 100 years, he would live 4,000 years. And science regards as fiction the Bible story that Adam lived 930 years.

Bernarr McFadden of Physical Culture Fame, believes that fasting will do for man, in a measure, what it does for worms. He writes:

"I have consistently maintained * * * that the body can be revived and made more youthful in every way, mentally, physically, etc., by fasting.

"It is my firm belief that we can live for an almost unlimited period, maybe for centuries, if the youth-building possibilities of a prolonged fasting process, followed by the use of nourishing elements that would fortify vitality, are properly investigated and understood in all their details."—Physical Culture Magazine, Aug. 1925.

A few years ago, Prof. Huxley, son of the elder Prof. Huxley, performed an experiment on young earth worms. He fed a family as they usually eat, except one worm, which he isolated and fed the same way, but now and then he made it fast. It was alternately fed and fasted.

The isolated worm was still alive and vigorous after 19 generations of its relatives had been born, lived their regular time, and died. Huxley explained the matter by stating that heavy eating clogs the life channels and hastens death.

Applying this procedure to man with similar results, instead of his dying at 100 and his friends thinking he had lived long, he would live almost 2,000 years. And science regards as fabulous the Biblical account that Methuselah lived 969 years.

Shall we believe God bestowed more power on worms than on man, the crowning work of Creation and Lord of the living world? That seems illogical.

In this instance, if a man who dies at 50 could extend his life-span 19 times, as in the case of the worm, he would live 950 years, the exact age of Noah (Gen. 9:29).

Is this coincidental, or does it reveal a secret of Nature known to the Ancient Masters? Did they understand the rejuvenating effect of a (1) controlled diet with (2) alternate fasting? We shall see.

FOUNTAIN OF YOUTH

Following this cue, Dr. H. M. Shelton says, *"The Fountain of Youth is within you"* (Orthobionomics, p. 291). Modern science has searched for it in all parts of the world, but never within the Body.

The Ancient Masters knew that within the body there actually flows a *River of Living Water* (John 7:38). Ancient Science knew this thousands of years ago (Gen. 9:4). But modern science knew it not until 1618 A.D., then refused to believe it when told.

In 1618 the famous Dr. Harvey proclaimed his discovery of the circulation of the blood—

and the medical schools only scoffed and sneer-
ed.   Hume, the historian, states:

> "No physician in Europe who had reached the
> age of 40, ever to the end of his life adopted Harvey's
> doctrine of the circulation of the blood." (Wilder,
> History of Medicine, p. 204).

With the death of Noah the knowledge of
the circulation of the blood seems to have been
lost, and ages later the ancient Greeks believed
the arteries were air tubes because they found
them empty in the dead body, and they were
named "artere" from "air."

This belief continued until the time of Harvey, who discovered the arteries did not carry
air, as taught by medical schools, but were
tubes filled with blood during life, and empty
only after death had fully drained their con-
tents into the veins.

The doctors were content to ridicule Harvey
at first; but when they began to realize they
were not able to disprove his statement, they
were filled with rage, and organized a system
of persecution against him, until it is said they
broke his heart (Dr. Wm. H. Hay).

Blinded by false theories unto this day,
medical schools cannot see the Fountain of
Youth when it stares them in the face. Their
work shows they search not for Truth and consider nothing that fails to support their pre-
conceived belief, founded on a false premise

They hide their ignorance in the darkness of
a dead language, and the multitude is mes-
merized by that which it cannot understand.

The Ancient Masters not only knew of the
circulation of the blood, but asserted that *"the
life of all flesh is the blood thereof"* (Gen.
9:4). At another time they wrote:

> "The life of the flesh is in the blood. It (blood)
> is the life of all flesh. The blood of it is for the life
> thereof. For the life of all flesh is in the blood
> thereof." (Lev. 17:11, 14).

Behold the striking repetition of a Basic
Principle of Nature in order to make a lasting
impression of a fundamental fact.

LAW OF DISEASE AND CURE

The Vital Fluid is the River of Living
Water, the Fountain of Youth. It turns the
Wheels of Life, and is the Rejuvenator of the
flesh. It is composed of what man breathes,
drinks and eats. By these functions he replen-
ishes the River of Living Water, which gives
him control of the condition of the Vital
Stream. The Fountain of Youth is what he
makes it; and from the magic power of its
silent chemistry there issues forth either good
health or bad depending on man's living habits.
Man reaps as he sows (Gal. 6:7).

This basic knowledge the Ancient Masters
possessed for ages, and used it effectively to
rejuvenate the body, and prolong life. By their

work they proved their wisdom. They taught
that—

    1. Disease results from stagnated circulation
and vitiated blood.

    2. Purification of the blood and acceleration
of its circulation is scientific cure.

    3. The means to accomplish this are supplied
only by the body.

    4. The body makes blood and purifies it.
Nothing else can do this vital work. The wisest
chemist cannot make one drop of blood.

    5. The supply determines the method of procedure.

    6. The procedure must be natural to be
favorable.

    7. Being natural, results are positive and
permanent.

This is the Ancient Law of Disease and
Cure. It made an exact science of the ancient
art of healing. Details of this law were concealed from the multitude. The law was never
known to the doctors of Europe, and is not
known now to the medical schools of this country.

During the Dark Ages of Europe (450 to
1550 A.D.), when the people there sank almost
to the Stone Age in ignorance, and even kings
could neither read nor write, that land was
swept with epidemics which the doctors could
not handle. The doctors can do but little better
now. The "flu-epidemic" of 1918 swept this
country with disease and death, and swept the

doctors off their feet. ·They were helpless and admitted it.

Experience shows that the object of medical schools is to perpetuate a certain system of thought, and nothing more. They know but little now about the body's functions, and previous to the modern discovery of the circulation of its fluids, they knew much less.

Until Harvey made that discovery the modern world was without a fundamental principle upon which to base any attempt to rejuvenate the body. This knowledge is still so new, that medical schools are in darkness on the subject of rejuvenation.

It is now known the blood is a vast transportation system, with many functions. It carries new material to all parts of the body to repair and renew its constantly decaying cells, and carries off for elimination their waste and excretory products.

This recently discovered knowledge proves the River of Living Water is the Fountain of Youth, by which every part of the body, every hour of its life, is incessantly repaired, renewed, rejuvenated, from the softest cell to the hardest bone. That is Regeneration in every sense of the word.

This newly discovered knowledge the medical schools know not how to use, and the puzzled doctors are asking, why does the body grow old and die?   Why should it not go on forever?

The great Metchnikoff was jeered by his medical brethren when he answered these questions. He declared that deterioration of bodily structure and old age are due to minute quantities of poisonous substances in the blood.

His work furnished the first logical explanation in modern times of the degenerative changes that occur in the body, and why. His findings have been confirmed by research workers, including Dr. George W. Crile, Dr. James Empringham, and Dr. Alexis Carrel.

1.   Crile says: "There is no natural death. All deaths from so-called natural causes are merely the end-point of a progressive acid saturation."

2.   Empringham says: "All creatures automatically poison themselves. Not Time, but these toxic products (in the blood) produce the senile changes we call old age."

3.   Carrell, famous biologist of the Rockefeller Institute, asserts: "The cell is immortal. It is merely the fluid in which it floats that degenerates. Renew this fluid at proper intervals, and give the cell nourishment upon which to feed, and, so far as we know, the pulsation of life may go on forever . . . Quickly, involuntarily, the thought comes: Why not with man? Why not purge the body of the worn-out fluids, develop a similar technique for renewing them—and so win immortality?"

How simple!   That process suggested by Carrel was followed by the Ancient Masters. They knew the River of Living Water is the

Fountain of Youth, the purpose of which is to sustain the body and maintain its integrity.

But every power that builds, also destroys upon a reversal of the lever. And so the body receives its death-blow from the blood due to man's evil work.

The blood is replenished, renewed, several times each day. But with what? Here is the root of the problem: The Fountain of Youth is renewed with foul air, impure water, decaying food, intoxicants, soda fountain slops, tea, coffee, chocolate, tobacco-juice, nicotine, and all that filthy substance of civilization which enter the lungs and stomach—and in time man dies *"of a progressive acid saturation."*

A startling discovery! Regeneration is a scientific fact! The discovery is so new that its possibilities have not even begun to be realized.

Old age and early death are due to poisons in the blood, says Metchnikoff—and his stupid medical brethren jeered. Purge the blood of its poisons and it becomes the Fountain of Youth in essence. The Ancient Masters knew whereof they spoke when they said:

"Thy youth shall be renewed like the eagle's." (Ps. 103:5).

Medical schools have never investigated the body's Rejuvenative Processes. But Naturo-

logists are making strides in that direction.   H.
Carrington describes the matter as follows:

> "The moment the last morsel of food is digest-
> ,ed and the stomach is emptied, a reconstruction
> process begins—a new tissue formation, owing to
> the fact that the broken-down cells are being replac-
> ed by (new) healthy ones; which is Nature's way
> of repairing any destroyed or injured part of the
> body.
> "This replacement of cells means replacement
> of tissue; replacement of tissue means a new stom-
> ach has been constructed—a stomach NEW in every
> sense of the word, as new in every anatomical
> sense as is the filling in of wounds, or between the
> fractured ends of bones." (Vitality, Fasting & Nutri-
> tion, p. 490).

Now we see why worms live so long under
alternate feeding and fasting.   The rejuvenative process begins not until after "the stomach is emptied."   No medical school has yet
discovered that fact.

Now we know why man sinks so rapidly
into decay and death.   Medical schools don't
know it, but the custom of eating three to six
and seven times a day, gives the burdened
stomach no chance to empty itself and repair
its worn and wasted cells.

It is not strange that civilization is cursed
with stomach and bowel complaints, with indigestion and constipation.   How do doctors
treat these ailments?   They give the poor patients poison called medicine, and feed them
more food.   We shall come to this again.

LAND OF CENTENARIANS

According to statistics, little Bulgaria, in southeastern Europe on the Black Sea, is the land of Centenarians in the civilized world. The Ency. Americana says:

"The climate (of Bulgaria) is healthy, and the country enjoys the reputation of possessing more centenarians than any other in Europe. People·said to be 105 to 125 years of age are not uncommon. * * * Over 70 per cent of the people are engaged in agriculture. * * * Fruits and vegetables are raised in abundance. * * * Wine is plentiful and cheap." —vol. 5, 1938, p. 1.

In 1927 a commission of Bulgarian doctors visited a large number of these old people, and reported they lived on a frugal fare of fruits, vegetables and milk products, usually sour milk and buttermilk; that they are lean to the point of being underweight, according to medical standards. Only one of the group was found to weigh as much as 168 pounds, the majority weighing between 122 and 130 pounds. They are industrious. Their habit is early to bed-and-early to rise, and to sleep uncovered as much as possible. Almost all of them are farmers and live in the open air and sunshine.

Every investigation reveals the dangers of high living and excessive eating. While Bulgaria has 58 centenarians per 100,000 of population, in the United States, the land of abundancy and gluttony, of intemperance and debauchery, of doctors and drugs, of vaccines and serums, we can boast of but four centenarians per 100,000 of population, with the number steadily declining.

There is no mystery surrounding the conditions of vigorous health and long life. Narrow is the way, and few there be that find it (Mat. 7:14). Simplicity, Frugality and Self-Denial are the sign-posts pointing to the Path of the Glorious Life (1 Cor. 9:25).

DIETETIC IGNORANCE OF DOCTORS

The multitude looks to the doctors, and the doctors admit they don't know.

Many conscientious persons lead a righteous life in all things but eating. They go wrong in eating and in the choice of foods because they follow the foolish advice of the doctors.

Experience shows that doctors know practically nothing about food and feeding, and some frankly admit it. The rest might as well, for their work discloses their ignorance.

These things are well known, and have often been published by leaders in the health field. Dr. K. Bain of the U. S. Children's Bureau, is reported in the press of October 24, 1941, as addressing the American Dietetic Association in session in St. Louis, and telling the group that —

"A stumbling block in medical education is the weak nutrition training of doctors and nurses."

Why this "stumbling block"? Because medical schools have consistently refused to recognize the fact that there is any relation between diet and disease. For how can food be the cause of disease when the medical world holds that disease is the work of germs? And how can disease be cured except by the use of poisons and serums to kill the "germs"?

It was the dietitians, not the doctors, who carried on their work, in the face of bitter medical ridicule, which brought to light the startling discovery that it is not Proteins, Fats and Carbohydrates which play the important part in nutrition, as taught by the medical world, but the elusive, little-known and less understood elements now called Vitamins and Mineral Salts.

The doctors and the controlled press worked hard to laugh and ridicule this discovery into oblivion. But the consistent results obtained by dietitians in feeding certain food to the sick were so amazing, that the multitude has grown food-conscious in spite of the cries of quackery and fraud by the doctors.

The marvelous experiments with the worms show the dangers of being what the doctors call "well-fed." If you are well-fed, you are on your way to early decrepitude and early death.

When the worms were well-fed, they grew fast. No doctor would condemn that, for that is the condition for which the doctors are striving. Feed children freely to make them grow fat and fast.

Behold the results. See how little the doctors know. The well-fed worms grew fast, they reached maturity fast, they began to decline fast, and they died fast.

But no orthodox doctor would attribute food and fast growth as the underlying cause of early decay and early death in man.

LAW OF ANALOGY

Man is not a worm. No. But his body is subject to the same law. Therefore, a worm has some analogy to or with a man. The analogy is legitimate and natural. It is valuable as pointing out the Path to the Glorious Life.

Scholars have recognized the value of analogy. Prof. W. Stanley Jevons, University College, London, writes:

> "The whole value of science consists in the power which it confers upon us of applying to one object, knowledge acquired from like objects; and it is only so far as we can discover and register resemblances that we can turn our observations to account. * * *
> "Whoever wishes to acquire a deep acquaintance with Nature must observe there are analogies which connect whole branches of science in a parallel manner, and enables us to infer of one class of phenomena what we know of another. It has happened on several occasions that the discovery of an unsuspected analogy between two branches of know-

ledge has been the starting-point for a rapid course of discovery.". (Principles of Science, 6. 631).

There is no branch of Science from which difficulties have not been removed by the certainties of a kindred branch, when analogically compared with it, or which, on similar comparisons, does not furnish new hints and valuable illustrations.

The result of the experiment with the worms constrains us to turn to the Biblical account of the early patriarchs. They did not develop fast; they did not grow old fast; they did not die fast.

Adam was 130 when he begat his first child, and he lived 930 years (Gen. 5:3,5). Methuselah was 187 when he begat his first child, and he lived 969 years (Gen. 5:25,27).

Then comes a startling change. Noah lived 950 years, but his grandson, Arphaxed, who begat his first child at the early age of 35, lived only 438 years (Gen. 11:12,13).

Peleg, great grandson of Arphaxed, begat his first child at 30, and died at the age of 239 (Gen. 11:18,19).

Nahor, only eight generations after Noah, begat his first child at the age of 29, and lived only 148 years (Gen. 11:24,25).

Man now grows faster; he reaches maturity faster; and he dies faster. Behold this law of

Nature. Here lies a great secret. Science has never tried to fathom it, because Science regards the stories in Genesis as fiction.

It is fair to infer from Biblical statements, that in the time of Adam and Noah, it required 100 years for man to reach maturity, and he lived nearly 1000 years, John Gardner, M.D., of England, in his book on Longevity, writes:

> "Before the Flood, men are said to have lived 500 and even 900 years. As a physiologist, I can assert positively there is no fact reached by science to contradict or render this improbable. It is more difficult, on scientific grounds to explain why man dies at all, than to believe in the duration of human life for a thousand years."

THE GREAT CHANGE

Dr. Walter says that under the same conditions the same result is obtained, and under a change of conditions, it is evident there must be a corresponding change of results.

As we review the lives of the patriarchs thru the ten generations from Adam to Noah inclusive, and the eight generations after Noah, a remarkable change appears in the length of the life-span.

The life-span from Adam to Noah inclusive. averaged 912 years. Adam lived 930 years, and Noah died at the age of 950.

There now comes a change. The life-span
from Noah's son Shem to Nahor, inclusive,
averaged only 345 years. Shem lived 602 years,
and Nahor died at the early age of 148.

The life-span of Shem was 348 years shorter
than Noah's, his father (Gen. 11:11). That
was the first appreciable decrease from the days
of Adam; and there was a reason for it.

While the medical world holds that such
things just happen, law and logic do not support that view. Under the same conditions the
same result is obtained. That is the law.

Passing to Nahor, only eight generations
after Noah, the life-span decreased to the short
period of 148 years (Gen. 11:25). An amazing
decline of 802 years in a few generations, as
previously stated.

We saw what happened to the worms when
well-fed. We saw the rejuvenating effect of the
(1) controlled diet combined with (2) alter-
nating fasting.

Is this the formula of Perpetual Youth that
Noah took with him when he passed into the
Great Beyond? Have we discovered the reason
why the life-span declined so fast after his
time?

BEING WELL FED

The experiment with the worms undoubted-
ly reveals, in part at least, the changed condi-

tions that caused the changed results in the life-span of the ancient patriarchs.

There must have been a change in food and feeding. Men must have been well fed, and they grew fat and fast, as do the foolish people of the U. S.

The experiment with the worms shows the result of being well-fed, and of growing fat and fast. It reveals the secret why the Ancient Masters so consistently taught the virtues of Simplicity, Frugality and Self-denial.

Ages of experience is showing, that a man created to himself new wants and a plentiful food supply, his health declined and his life-span decreased. We find that—

1. The dawn of Man pictures him in a friendly climate, where he is naked and not uncomfortable, satisfying his hunger with the delicious fruits of vines and trees, growing in a garden that he was ordered to dress and to keep. (Gen. 2:7,25).

2. Then, in addition to these fruits, he turns to herbs and vegetables, which he obtained from a more avaricious earth, as the reward of his work.

3. He next domesticates wild beasts and drinks as milk the excrements of their blood. This is the beginning of the beastly development in man. For Like begets Like.

4. Lastly, he slays the dumb brutes and feasts on their festing flesh. This is the beginning of hybridism in man. For "Man is what he eats," declares Dr. W. H. Manwaring, prof. of bacteriology and pathology, Stanford University, Calif.

PHYSIOLOGICAL REST

We know the value of rest. Fasting means Rest for the vital organs. The Ancient Scientists knew the value of resting the vital organs. Modern science may make that discovery some day. But it will not happen so long as modern science continues to believe in the theory that Life and Energy come from Food.

Fasting and frugal eating is the Path to the Glorious Life. Frugal eating nourishes the body without overworking the internal organs. Fasting gives these organs needed rest. We saw what this means in the case of the worms. The body of man is subject to the same law.

The ancient master recognized Fasting as the Great Remedial Measure, and resorted to it in instances of illness. The measure was also employed generally to improve human health, and the rules, by official edict, pro-claimed periodic fasts throughout their realms (2 Chron. 2:03). The Bible states:

"The word of the Lord of hosts came unto me saying: The Fast of the fourth month, and the fast of the fifth, and the fast of the sixth, and the fast of the seventh, and the fast of the tenth, shall be to the house of Judah joy and gladness." (Zech. 8-19).

Fasting twice in the week was a common custom in the days of Jesus (Lu. 18:12). The disciples of John fasted often (Lu. 5:33). David fasted (2 Sam. 12:16) and so did Ahab (1 Ki. 21:27). Moses fasted forty days (Ex.

34.28). Elijah fasted forty days (1 Ki. 19:8).
Jesus fasted forty days (Mat. 4:2). These wise
men knew how to promote health and prolong
life. They knew that doctors and drugs possess
no magic nor healing power.

SCIENCE OF REJUVENATION

Modern man knows nothing about Rejuvenation. Modern science knows so little about it
that it cannot discuss the subject intelligently.
Much evidence appears in the writings of the
Ancient Masters to show they thoroughly understood the matter.

Until Harvey discovered the circulation of
the blood, the Process of Rejuvenation was
unknown to modern science, and it was considered the height of ignorance for one to
suggest the possibility of Rejuvenation.

Previous to Harvey's discovery, medical
schools knew so little about the body's functions that they had no fundamental principle
upon which to base an attempt to prolong
human life.

Out of Harvey's discovery came that knowledge which has led to some progress in this
field. But the body's functions are still so little
understood, that doctors are not qualified to
conduct properly the Process of Rejuvenation.
As a result of this incompetency—

"Not even one day has been added to the span of human life," says the great scientist Carrel, who adds:

"A man of 45 has no more chance of dying at the age of 80 now, than in the last century . . . "

"Science follows no plan . . . Men of science know not where they are going . . . We shall have to go farther and build up a real science of man . . . The science of man is still too rudimentary to be useful." (Man, The Unknown, pp. 23, 42, 178, 179).

Here is a medical leader declaring the medical world knows next to nothing about Man.

This profound ignorance of the doctors is proven by the fact, that the best of them die at early ages. Before us lies the daily paper of Nov. 20, 1941, with the account that Dr. Richard C. Foster, president of the University of Alabama, *"died tonight of creeping paralysis,"* at the age of 46.

With few doctors living to reach the century mark, with most of them dying in their early years, it should be expected of them to sneer the Biblical statement that the Ancient Masters lived 900 years.

Before Harvey's discovery, medical schools knew not that Vital Force, under the Law of Change, is constantly engaged in tearing down the old and worn tissues, and rebuilding them again of new material supplied by the "river of life." How can such a machine wear out?

It has been only within the last 50 or 60 years that medical schools knew that all cells, tissues and organs of the body are always renewed by the Fountain of Youth, and always ready to perform their alloted work.

When the discovery was made that the River of Life is actually the Fountain of Youth within the body, the doctors, in astonishment, quickly inquired: Why does the body grow old and die?

To find the answer, feverish research has been done, and this is the reply:

1. "There is no physical reason at the present day why man should die." (Dr. Wm. A. Hammond, late Surgeon, U.S. Army).

2. "With a perfectly balanced endocrine system, man would live forever. In fact, your Fountain of Youth is within yourself." (Dr. Friedenburg, noted physician of New York).

3. "The human frame as a machine is perfect. It contains within itself no marks by which we can possibly predict its decay. It is apparently intended to go on forever." (Dr. Munroe).

The Ancient Masters knew how to make the River of Life the Fountain of Youth. But they kept the secret concealed from the multitude, and have been careful to leave no complete outline of it.

A few advanced physiologists, losing faith in the "practice of medicine" and looking in other fields for the Elixir of Life, have at last discovered that secret by piecing together their findings, and comparing them with ancient writings.

Their first discovery was so simple it amazed them. They found that all animals, when ill, refuse to eat. Here is a law of Nature, said they. The teaching of medical schools is diametrically opposed to it. They insist on feeding patients "plenty of good, nourishing food to keep up their strength."

Strength comes from food, say the medical schools, and stupid man so believes. But strength comes not to the invalid, no matter how well fed; while the brawny athlete gains in strength as he prepares for his performance on one scanty meal a day, and reduces his weight considerably.

The physiologists did more thinking. They observed the (1) high death-rate under regular medical procedure of feeding patients well, and they grew more skeptical.

They studied (2) the cases of animals that invariably fast when ill, and almost always recovered health. This law of Nature works, said they.

Then they studied (3) the writings of the Ancient Masters and found frequent references to fasting. The Ancient Masters knew the law.

Lastly, they noticed the Ancient Masters never (4) filled their stomach with food when preparing for unusual events. They always fasted. They not only knew the law, but obeyed it.

With this valuable evidence to guide them, they began to experiment on worms, with results so favorable that they turned to man. Always were the same good results obtained.

By fasting their patients, the recoveries were so remarkable as to be amazing. In their enthusiasm they called it the "Wonder Cure." It was tried by Dr. Adolph Mayer, an eminent German physician, and he wrote:

"I assert that fasting is the most efficient means for correcting disease." (Fast Cure — Wonder Cure).

Dr. Moeller, superintendent of the Closchwitz sanitarium, said:

"Fasting is the only natural evolutionary method whereby, through a systematic cleansing, the body can restore itself by degrees to physiological normality."

As disease is degeneration, reasoned the physiologists, a procedure that consistently cures disease and restores the body's normal physiology, must be a Process of Regeneration. And they are right.

That is how leading physiologists stumbled onto the Law of Regeneration.

The Bible shows that when preparing for extraordinary events, the Ancient Masters always fasted. They knew by experience that fasting improved their physical and quickened their mental powers.

The case of the worms and the findings of modern physiologists prove they were right. Their work shows they were not psuedo-scientists, as we have today, but true scientists of the first water.

Delving deeper into the subject, these physiologists found that constant and heavy eating is the path to disease and premature death. That explains the high death-rate of doctors, who practice what they are taught and die early as a result.

The custom of eating from three to six and seven times a day sends man into disease, degeneration and early death. The body becomes burdened with more material than it can use. The surplus creates a dangerous condition. It stagnates the "river of life," damages the delicate machinery, clogs the life-channels, and saturates the whole system with deadly toxins.

1. What did Dr. Empringham say? "All creatures automatically poison themselves."

2. What did Dr. Crile say? "All deaths are merely the end-point of a progressive acid saturation."

3. What did the great scientist Metchnikoff say? "Deterioration of bodily structures and old age are due to poisonous substances in the blood." And his dumb medical brethren jeered.

Physiologists show that man, by his living habits, makes his blood the (1) sparkling river of life, or the (2) stagnant stream of death.

Investigation shows that as waste and toxins accumulate in the blood, the delicate cells become flooded with filth and choked and poisoned by their own excrement which the overworked organism is unable to eliminate.

Many of the cells decay and die. All of them are more or less damaged. The person becomes ill. He is frightened. He thinks he is going to die, and calls a doctor. What does the doctor know? Ask Metchnikoff. They jeered him when he explained the cause of disease, decay and old age.

That is disease. That is how disease is built. That is why the body sinks into degeneration and early death. That is the Ancient Secret. That is the broad highway modern man travels in ignorance, as he follows his blind leaders, the dumb doctors who jeered the great Metchnikoff when he explained the cause of decay and old age.

Ask yourself this question: Can disease be cured by giving patients medicine and more food? God forbid. Do you wonder why pa-

tients so treated so often fail to recover? Do
you see why patients so treated die while yet
in the flower of youth? Medical ignorance of
the body's functions is the answer.

Upton Sinclair knew something of the virtues of Fasting. He wrote:

> The great thing about the Fast is that it sets
> you a new standard of health."

In spite of the fact that man follows a faulty
course of living in most respects, and seldom
concords with the law of his being, the constant
renewal of the cells by the "river of life" holds
old age at bay for a considerable period of
time. That is the reason why some men live
for a century in spite of bad habits, and without knowing a thing about the Law of Life or
the body's processes.

> 1. Fasting rejuvenates because it permits the
> "river of life" to flow freely, thus allowing the re-
> newal processes to exceed those of disintegration.
> 2. Fasting enables the depurative organs to
> purge the "river of life" of toxins, and the body of
> diseased, worn out, and low grade tissues.
> 3. Fasting permits the body to clean house,
> purify its fluids, normalize its chemistry, and regain
> its proper equilibrium. That is Regeneration.

The rejuvenation effect of Fasting was
known to the Ancient Masters. It is positive
and certain, and so evident as to be readily
observed. The effects are visible in the external parts of the body, and in the function of

the sensory organs. Sight, smell, hearing, taste and touch all show marked improvement. The sense of smell, for instance, improves so much the faster is often nauseated by foul odors that are usually unnoticed by him.

Prof. Sergius Morgulis, Nebraska College of Medicine, wrote a masterly work entitled "Fastings & Undernutrition," in which he relates specific instances of Rejuvenescence thru Fastings. He states:

"The acuity of the senses" is increased by fasting, and "at the end of his 31 days' abstinence from food, Prof. Levanzin could see twice as far as he could at the beginning of the fast."

There is more proof. Under the process of fasting, wrinkles, pimples and blotches disappear, and the skin regains its youthful appearance. The same regenerative effect takes place in all organs and glands. Dr. H. M. Shelton says.

"The fasting body begins to grow small, and in order to maintain the integrity of its vital organs, it utilizes all the surplus material it has on hand. Growths, deposits, effusions, dropsical swellings, infiltrations, fat, etc., are absorbed and used to support these organs.

"With no digestive drudgery on hand, Nature employs the long desired opportunity for general house cleaning purposes. Accumulations of surplus tissues are overhauled and analyzed; the available component parts are turned over to the department of nutrition, while the refuse is thoroughly and permanently removed." (Regeneration of Life, p. 93).

Under the rejuvenative effect of Fasting the River of Life is purged of its poisons and becomes the Fountain of Youth. Abnormal growths and dropsical swelling disappear, running sores heal, enlarged glands return to normal size, and the vital organs grow stronger, including weak hearts. H. Carrington writes:

"The fact that hitherto weak hearts are strengthened and cured by fasting, proves conclusively that any such unusual symptoms, observed during this period, denotes a beneficial reparative process." (Vitality, Fasting & Nutrition, p. 464).

Physiologists show that nerve energy, during a fast, is conserved and transmitted in more powerful waves to the vital organs, enabling them to improve in force and function, and to eliminate more fully the waste and toxins which accumulate under constant feeding.

"The degree of rejuvenescence" in such cases says Prof. Child, "is in general proportionate to the degree of re-organization in the process of reconstruction of the piece into a whole."

It is obvious that the degree of regeneration will not be so great in a decrepit man of 60 or 70 as in the case of that man at the age of 45 or 50.

Now for an amazing example in the case of man: Doctors Carlson and Kunde, University of Chicago, showed that a fast of 15 days temporarily restores the tissues of a man of 40 to the physiological condition (age) of those of a youth of 17.

Astounding! Not only does Fasting stop the onward march of physiological age for man like it does for worms, but it even turns back the hands of measuring Time for him like it does for worms.

We have found the Key of *The Ancient Secret* of regeneration, known to the Ancient Masters but concealed from the multitude (Mark 4:11). They spoke often of cases of rejuvenation, but their writings have not been understood. Now we can read their words with better understanding:—

> His flesh shall be fresh as a child's; he shall return to the days of his youth (Job 33:25). And thy youth shall be renewed like the eagle's (Ps. 103:5). These things worketh God oftentimes with man (Job 33:29).

Modern science has branded these biblical statements as fables and fiction. But advanced physiologists are proving the statements are true.

Fasting made the flesh of a man of 40 as fresh as that of a child's; and his youth was renewed like the eagle's.

That is exactly what the Ancient Masters wrote. But in our ignorance we could not understand, and refused to believe. To remain ignorant is to remain a slave (Wayland). Ignorance is the power that keeps man in darkness.

Under the process of fasting, a man of 40 regains 23 years of life. This means that a man of 64 in solar years, would be only 41 in physiological years. This explains why we, at the age of 74, feel in body and mind as we did in 1919.

On this test of Rejuvenation we base our belief that we still have 60 or 70 or even more years to live, barring accidents. One of our uncles recently died at 93, and he knew nothing about the Law of Life. Our lifetime study of the subject should enable us to outlive him 30 or 40 years.

In this respect we are encouraged by the fact, that it is harder to bring back the condition of youth when lost, than to keep from losing it. We keep it by living in harmony with the law. We have done that for forty years, and are as active and supple now as we were forty years ago.

An article in the press of Feb. 27, 1938, stated that Tapsi Bishan Das Udasi, of India, was reported to be 172 years old, but "appears to be not over 40." He claims to know the secret of rejuvenation but will tell no one.

The press of June 11, 1933, related the death of Li Ching-yun at the amazing age of 256. He was born in 1677 and had papers to show that he was congratulated by the Chinese Government on his 150th and 200th birthdays.

Sir William Temple states that the Brahmins of India, who live mostly on fruit and green herbs and drink only water, live to be 300 years old.

An item in the press in 1923 stated that Sadhu Swami, of Karinganji, India, was living then at the age of 330.

Peter Maffins, in his history of India, tells of Numas De Cugna who died in 1566 at the age of 370. His teeth, beard and hair were renewed four times—the work of regeneration.

Biologists assert that if the cells of a man of 40 can be regenerated to equal those of a youth of 17, it is possible to keep them indefinitely in that condition. If that is possible, then it is certainly within the limits of that possibility (V.S., p. 204).

By exhaustive experiments, Dr. Morgulis proved beyond the shadow of a reasonable doubt, that Fasting is a dependable process of regeneration, and the only one known to man. He found that during a fast the body does not tear down its tissues nor impair them structurally. The cells are merely reduced in size, as in the case of the worms. They decrease in bulk but not in number.

Strange to say, the nuclei of the cells lose so little bulk under a fast, that they become relatively larger in ratio to the rest of the cell, as in the case of children. And, as in the case of children, such cells have the same capacity for assimilation and growth which characterizes the cells of the young. This is further evidence that fasting rejuvenates, and accounts for the fast growth of tissue when feeding begins after fasting ends.

After the fast has purged the blood of toxins and the body of clogging waste and decaying and diseased cells, healthy cells are built of better material to replace those cast out of the body during the fast.

That is Regeneration. That is the secret of the Ancient Masters. Know the law and observe it. That is the way to keep your body active and vigorous.

In the days of Adam and Noah, man ate only the juice of fruits of Nature and drank the water of coconuts. They ate less in a day, perhaps, than modern man eats in one meal. The duration of their youth extended over several centuries (Gen. 5:32), and they lived almost a thousand years.

LOST HEALTH REGAINED

Many persons have sunk almost to the brink of the grave, as Cornaro did, and then turned to Nature after losing faith in doctors and their worthless methods, and not only regained health, but lived a long and useful life.

There is the case of John Bailes, of England, who suffered in middle life from a severe illness of a chronic nature, and was unable to find any doctor who could help him. The doctors told him he could not get well, and had only a short time to live. He turned to Nature, adopted a strict mode of living, and lived to be 128 years old.

Capt. Goddard E. Diamond, of San Francisco, at the age of 79 was suffering from a severe case of hardened tissues and blood-vessels, with stiffness of the joints. Yet for 30 years he had lived a life of what is called Vegetarianism.

The tissues of his legs and back were so hardened, that he could not rise from a chair nor sit down without extreme discomfort, and he often required the aid of an assistant. The tissues of his arms and hands were so stiff, that it was with difficulty that he held a knife and fork to feed himself.

The doctors being unable to give him relief, he turned to Nature, adopted a strict mode of living, and was still alive in 1915, at the age of 119, being born in 1796, while George Washington was still living, and had seen 29 presidents of the U.S.A. elected.

When Diamond was over 100 he was doing gymnastic work with an athletic club that few young men could equal. At the age 108 he rode a bicycle and walked 20 miles a day. He attended social events, and when he was 110 he once danced most of the night with an athletic girl of 16.

As cases of this kind come before us, we are prone to ponder the question of how long man could live, if he began to live properly from the start, and kept it up to the end.

It is a fact that a body once weakened by disease, will always remain below par. The scientist Carrel says, *"We bear forever the scar of those events."* (Man, The Unknown, p. 170).

While a diseased heart, liver, kidney, pancreas, stomach, etc., may be regenerated to such extent that it fails to bother its owner, and may give good service for years, such organ cannot again become normal. That fact is proven by the evidence that a wound, though it heals, yet leaves a scar composed of low grade tissue.

A fatty heart, a fibrous liver, a diseased mucous membrane—these can not return to their normal state. But as the original size of an external scar diminishes with the passage of time, so the diseased organs, by a process of strict living, will continue to improve with the passing of years.

PROCESS OF SCLEROSIS

Sclerosis means hardening and thickening of cells and tissues. This is the condition of decrepitude. It is due, in a large part, to deposits in blood-vessels, glands, tissues and cells. The deposits accumulate until a state of hardening occurs, and this is old age.

The symptoms of old age appear in ratio with the progress of hardening. If the body of a boy were stiffened in the same degree as that of a man of 80, the boy's body would show similar signs of age.

If it is possible to prevent hardening, it is possible to prolong youth and postpone old age. This can be done. The Ancient Scientists knew the secret.

Capt. Diamond's case supplies valuable data. After 30 years of vegetarianism, he is afflicted with general sclerosis. His diet, no doubt, consisted chiefly of cereals and cereal products. These contain large quantities of minerals that stiffen joints, tissues, and blood-vessels, "and as a class," writes Densmore, "are the worst adapted as food for man."

Bread, "man's so-called 'staff of Life,' is, to a great extent, the cause of premature death," continues Densmore (p. 290), who adds:

"Dr. Rowbotham, of England, adduced proof in his work published 50 years ago, that cereal foods

tend to the ossification (hardening) of joints and
tissues, and to produce decreptitude and early death"
(Natural Food of Man, p. 390).

Densmore adds that the same conclusions
have been reached independently by leading
doctors of England, France and Germany. Dr.
C. C. Hibbs, in an article on Dental Decay,
says:

> "The grains are responsible for nearly all of
> man's disease, for wheat, oats, rye, and barley are
> no more a part of man's food than oranges the food
> of a cow, or grass the food of cats . . .
>
> "Eliminate grains from the diet, and decay in
> children's teeth will cease. Tarter and pyorrhea
> will disappear. The hospitals will fold up, and
> medicine will be a dream. All the doctors on earth
> with their 'vast' medical experience cannot disprove
> this statement.
>
> "The medical profession dare not take a group
> of children and feed them according to Nature's
> law for six months, then truly publish the results."
> (You Can't Eat That).

Cereals and cereal products constitute the
basis of modern man's food. Knight, in his
"Food of Man," states that early man could
not have known of cereals, pulses and starchy
vegetables; that the cereals have been developed from grass plants now unknown to Botan-
ists; and that tropical regions, the natural
home of man, are filled with the luxuriance of
Nature's provision for man in the way of lus-
cious fruits. (Densmore, p. 393).

The case of Capt. Diamond shows the process of sclerosis can be halted not only, but its evil effects largely removed by proper living.

A person affected with sclerosis should begin the rejuvenation process with a fast, drinking only water, live in the sunshine and pure air, take all the exercise he can with comfort, and a sweat bath every day.

CASES OF FASTING

Most people never fasted and are afraid to try it. Medical doctors, groping in the dark, foolishly assert it is dangerous to go six or seven days without food. Nothing better could be expected of a group of misguided persons who believe that building health is the same as the process of fattening hogs.

In thousands of fasts, ranging from thirty to 100 days, no deaths have been known to occur that could be attributed to the fast.

The press of January 14, 1937, states that Dr. S. H. Tanner, Minneapolis physician, abstained from food for 40 days in 1880, to settle an argument with a colleague of the New York Neurological society.

For 18 days Tanner took neither food nor water. Then he began drinking from 40 to 70 ounces of water every 24 hours. When the fast ended, Tanner had lost 35 pounds, but suffered no ill effects. His pulse and temperature remained almost normal throughout the fast.

The press of May 2, 1937, reported that Jackson Whitlow, a religious zealot, fasted 35 days. His wife stated that he refused food "on the Lord's orders." His weight dropped to 92 pounds, but he suffered no ill effects.

The press of August 13, 1938, stated that Mrs. Mae Zimmerman fasted 63 days to gain relief from the pains of arthritis. She. lost 38 pounds.

Mary Mitchell, age 27, Santa Ana, Calif., a practical nurse, in January, 1927, broke a fast of 64 days. She weighed 202 pounds when the fast began, and 158 when it ended.

For the first five weeks of the fast, she continued her work as nurse, and during the remainder of the fast, she worked about her home, preparing food for members of the family, and said this did not tempt her to eat. Her health and energy were much improved by the fast.

In June, 1926, George H. Johnson walked from Chicago to Bald Knob, Pa., without food. covering the 578 miles in 20 days in a contest to win a prize. He said he was in fine condition when the journey ended.

Maybell Collins of South Africa fasted 101 days in 1931 to reduce, according to the press. She weighed 232 pounds when the fast began, and 169 when it ended. She said she was in good health, went out to parties and carried on with her public singing.

An English business man, age 53, who refused to permit the use of his name, began a fast October 30, 1932, under the care of John W. Armstrong, who has conducted hundreds of fasts. He took nothing but water until 6:30 p.m. Feb. 7, 1933, a fast of 109 days. He could have continued 10 days more had it been necessary. His weight dropped from 191 to 132 pounds. He said he was on his "last legs"; that nothing did him any good. He tried fasting as a last resort, and regained health.

C. H. Cowan fasted for 42 days. When he began he weighed 165 pounds, and when the fast ended he weighed 135 pounds (Dewey, p. 118).

Milton Rathburn fasted 35 days. When he began he weighed 211 pounds and when the fast ended he weighed 168. He said: "I feel like a boy again. I think I could vault over a six foot fence." (Dewey, p. 126).

Miss Estella Kuenzel, age 22, lost her mental health to a degree that death became the final object of desire. A fast of 45 days restored her health. (Dewey, p. 140).

Leonard Thress, age 57, recovered his health by fasting 50 days. His weight dropped from 209 pounds to 133. He declared that all his ailments left and he never felt better. (Dewey, p. 149).

Elizabeth Westing, music teacher, in poor health, fasted 40 days. Her weight dropped

from 110 pounds to 93. On the last day of her
fast she was able to sing with unusual clear-
ness and power, and ended her fast without
losing a day from her duties as a teacher of
music. (Dewey, p. 155).

Dr. Edward H. Dewey, from whose work.
"The Fasting-Cure," we have excerpted the
last five cases above, considers excessive eating
such a curse, that he writes:

> "The ways of the kitchen and dining-room are
> the ways of disease and death, ways whose ends
> are prisons, asylums, scaffolds, to a far larger ex-
> tent than is dreamed of by the fathers and mothers
> of the land." (p. 182).

In the press of January 25, 1938, was an
account to the effect that for 10 years Giovanni
Succi traveled thru Europe giving exhibitions
of fasting. His exhibitions, severely controlled,
extended for periods of 30 to 40 days, during
which time he was in the public eye day and
night. Included were 80 periods of 30 days of
fasting, and 20 periods of 40 days of fasting—
a total of 3200 days of rigorous fasting.

There are 3650 days in 10 years of 365 days
per year. As Succi fasted 3200 days in the 10
years, he fasted eight years and 280 days.

ETERNAL LIFE

We hear much talk, in these days of deceptive propaganda, about what medical art has
done to improve man's health and increase his
life-span.

The great scientist, Alexis Carrel, M.D., in his book, "Man, The Unknown," 1935, makes this statement:

> "We (medical doctors) have not succeeded in increasing the duration of our (man's) existence. A man of 45 has no more chance of dying at the age of 80 now than in the last century.
>
> "This failure of hygiene and medicine is a strange fact. In spite of the progress achieved in the heating, ventilation, and lighting of houses, of dietary hygiene, bath-rooms, and sports, of periodical medical examinations, and increasing number of medical specialists, not even one day has been added to the span of human life." (p. 178).

That sums up the empty result of 3,000 years of medical work. What profit has it brought man? Yet it has cost civilization billions upon billions of dollars.

Mary E. Forbes wrote a book, copyright 1926, printed in Paris, France, in which she makes surprising statements that meet the test of law and logic. From this book we excerpt the following:

Prof. Monit, of Harvard, in his book, Age, Growth and Decay, says

> Death is not a universal accompaniment of life. In many of the lower organisms death does not occur so far as we know at present, as a natural necessary result of life. Death with them is purely the result of accident, some external cause. Our existing science leads us to the conclusion, therefore, that death has been acquired during the progress of evolution of living organisms."

So we find science supporting the Garden of Eden story, which tells in allegorical form that something man did evolved disease and death.

Ancient Scientists possessed the secret of longevity and perpetual youth. They lived in accordance with this knowledge before the Flood, and at 150 were still young, just beginning to have children. Methuselah was 187 when he begat his first son, and Noah was 500 when he had his first child (Gen. 5:20, 25, 28, 32).

Thomas Parr died at the age of 153. Dr. Harvey, modern discoverer of the circulation of the blood, performed an autopsy, and found his organic condition good. No signs of decay appeared in his organs or glands. His death was attributed to over-eating of rich food at the royal household of the King, who had invited him thither, as he wanted to learn from the most interesting of his subjects the secret of long life.

As the fierce, flesh-eating races from the West overwhelmed the peaceful fruitarians of the Far East, the secret how to preserve vitality and prolong life was concealed from the invaders, and for centuries afterwards was confined to a small group, handed down from generation to generation.

FUNCTION OF LIFE

The function of Life is to create, sustain and inhabit. Creation carries with it the power to sustain, and that which is sustained by Life should be immortal.

Life develops man to maturity. After that, the body should show no change to a downward trend.

Life is eternal. But it can be forced to withdraw from the form it has organized. When this occurs, the form disintegrates. But this withdrawal is not necessary nor inevitable.

If the function of Life is to create and develop man, to carry him on to maturity, and sustain him, it should not begin at that point to impair and destroy the body it has made.

Life would not be consistent with its purpose, if it deliberately and willfully destroyed that which it had created.

Having developed man from a speck, there is no reason known why Life should not maintain him for an indefinite period. Leading physiologists assert it would do so, if he obeyed the law. The end is hastened by the habit of trying to doctor and cure the Effects of transgression, instead of removing the Cause. In other words, the belief in the doctors is another factor that leads to early death.

Maud Levett writes:

"There will be no dust to return to dust when a better brain and a better knowledge of the properties of food and air will do away with the separation of man from his body."

Death is not natural. (If it were, it would not have been necessary for God to pass the

death sentence on man—Gen. 2:17). Death
does not inhere in living forms. There are organized forms of minerals, vegetables and animals that never die.

Death comes to all creatures that violate the
law, or have not the intelligence and capacity
to control and regulate their conduct and environment. These qualities man has, thus making him superior to all other animals.

Man may rise superior to his Environment
by reason of his great intelligence. He is competent to discover and abide in a favorable
Environment, and thus supply conditions that
would make him immortal.

The Bible says that man shall conquer
Death (1 Cor. 15:55). That idea is beginning
to take hold of thinking men.

With the capacity for Intelligence that would
make man a god, the small amount of intelligence developed is used to obstruct the operation of Life's function.

The body is subject to a law that takes no
account of Time. The same process that makes
the body old and withered, would, upon a
change of conditions, make it young and keep
it vigorous.

In the vegetable and animal world the ar-
rival at maturity, flowering, fruiting and decaying is a universal process which no one will
deny. But to hold this process applies with
equal force to man, is to deny his higher plane

of existence, and to see no difference between him, the master of himself and his environ- ment, and the beasts, which are ruled by appe- tite and passion, and are unable to command anything.

Man's body is subject to the law of matter, along with the birds and beasts. But he has a brain which, if developed, enables him to rise superior to the animal plane, and to supply conditions that transform degeneration into re- generation.

(This ends the excerpts from the book of Mary E. Forbes).

THE CHEMICAL BASIS

"The particular chemical composition of the body," writes Mary E. Forbes, "calls for food of like chemical composition." She says the medical world knows nothing about this fact The faulty work of doctors proves she is right.

In "The Science of Life," Wells and Huxley discuss Old Age under the heading: "The Wearing Out of the Machine." They say in part:

"The chemical basis of this wearing out is at present not understood Old Age seems to be as- sociated in some way with defective calcium metabol- ism. The brittleness of senescent bones is due to the reabsorption of lime salts into the blood. More- over, there seems to be an accumulation of poison- ous substances in the blood. * * * Sooner or later one or the other of the essential organs fails and the body dies.

"It is important to realize that our cells do not die because mortality is inherent in their internal structure. They die because they are parts of a very complicated system based on co-operation, and sooner or later one of the tissues lets the others down. * * *

"As a matter of fact, living matter is potentially immortal. If one keeps a culture from the tissues of a young animal and takes sub-cultures regularly, the race of cells can apparently go on growing and dividing indefinitely.

"Death is a consequence of incomplete organization. The tissues die because they are parts of an imperfectly balanced body.

"How long it may be possible for a body to sustain its balance and continue indefinitely, or at least for a much longer period than the common life of its species, is an interesting matter for speculation."

"The tissues die because they are parts of an imperfectly balanced body," asserts Wells and Huxley. Be it so, but the imperfect balance is the fault of man, not of the body.

The (1) Power to establish and the (2) Mechanism to maintain a perfect balance in all departments of the body, is inherent in the organism, and requires no aid from doctors or nurses.

The body needs only to be permitted to operate unhampered in order to preserve its equilibrium. The process of repair and renewal is automatic in operation; and science has shown that it is capable of continuing indefinitely, unless hindered by man's faulty habits.

Experience shows that man's mode of living has become so faulty and so foreign to the Law of Life, that he begins to decline almost as soon as he attains maturity, and often before; and he sinks down in death when he should be in his prime.

SUMMARY

1.   The findings of science support the parable of the Garden of Eden, showing that what man does to himself is the Cause of disease and death (Gen. 2:17).

2.   The evidence shows the ancient patriarchs knew how to live to preserve the body and prolong its youthfulness. Methuselah was 187 when he begat his first child, and he lived 969 years (Gen. 5:25,26).

3.   There can be no deterioration in a body (a) sustained by Eternal Life and (b) maintained in perfect balance and repair by the River of Life.

4.   The chemical composition of the body demands material of the same chemical composition from the River of Life. Such material is natural, unheated, uncooked and unseasoned food, as produced by Nature, and pure air.

5.   Medical schools are ignorant of this law, and recommend substances detrimental to the body, resulting in changes in the body's chemistry, which produce imperfect balance, decay and death.

6. Modern science says, "The chemical basis of this wearing out (of the body) is not understood." The Ancient Masters possessed this knowledge and used it to preserve youth and prolong life.

7. Science shows that living matter is potentially immortal, and subject to a law that takes no account of Time. The cells die not because mortality inheres in them, but because of chemical changes and accumulations of poisons, which produce an imperfectly balanced body.

8. Death is the sequel of faulty organization, arising from the faulty work of man, done usually in ignorance, and due to lack of knowledge of the Law of Life.

9. These secrets the Ancient Masters knew, and taught in the schools of the Ancient Sacred Mysteries, of which Apollonius was an initiate.

10. Simplicity, Frugality and Self-Denial are the primary qualities that constitute the Path of the Glorious Life.

11. The less physical Man becomes thru the conquest of his Passions and Desires, the less he needs. The less Man needs, the more he can become like gods, who use nothing and are immortal.

He that overcometh shall inherit all things (Rev. 21:7). Few men there be in civilization who have the Will Power to overcome the twin demons, Passion and Desire (Mat. 7:14).

PART 2.

Key To Vital Energy

SYMPTOMS OF CO POISONING

DIAGNOSIS: That part of medicine whose object is the discrimination of disease, and the knowledge of the pathognomonic signs of each. It is one of the most important branches of general pathology. (Med. Dict.)

SYMPTOMS: Any change, perceptible to the senses, in any organ or function, which is connected with morbific influences. It is by the aggregate and succession of symptoms that a disease is detected. (Med. Dict.)

In simple language for the layman, diagnosis is nothing more nor less than the searching out, studying and naming the symptoms of Impaired Health, erroneously calling them "diseases," and treating them as dangerous entities per se. That deceptive, illusory, confusing system is boastingly termed "medical science." Ages of experience show that in truth and in fact it is pure medical nonsense.

Impaired Health does exhibit certain symptoms, but disregarding the CAUSE lying back of the symptoms while treating the symptoms as dangerous entities, is not the proper, natural and scientific way to relieve the condition of bad health or build the condition of good health.

That the misled layman may have a better picture of this medical illusion, we shall consider some of the Symptoms of Carbon Monoxide Poisoning. Beck called attention to the fact that certain so-called diseases are but the symptoms of slow carbon monoxide asphyxiation. These symptoms he found to be chiefly: headache, dizziness, nervousness, nerve and muscle pains, digestive disturbances, fatigue, restlessness, depressed feeling, shortness of breath, palpitation. Other symptoms were mental confusion, difficulty in talking, symptoms of stomach ulcer, anemia, hyperemia and typical angina pectoris.

All these "symptoms of diseases" disappeared, some very promptly, when nothing more was done than to remove the patients into pure air, free of carbon monoxide gas.

Most frequent symptoms of the effect of CO poisoning are tightness across the forehead, headache, dilatation of the cutaneous blood vessels, fatigue, muscular weakness, dizziness, impairment of vision and hearing, nausea, vomiting, and collapse. These symptoms are hastened and intensified by exercise in air containing CO, due to deeper breathing and greater inhalation of the polluted air.

Quite often the appearance of the victim is that of one with alcoholic intoxication. The eyes may appear dull, more or less fixed, and somewhat bulging. The character of the respiration changes—the rate is first increased. and later slowed and irregular.

When birds are exposed to carbon monoxide gas they appear moribund. They show signs of distress when exposed for 60 minutes to air containing 0.1 per cent of CO. and for 2 to 5 minutes to 0.2 per cent CO.

When Dr. J. S. Haldane, in his experiment on himself, breathed air containing 0.12 per cent of CO. he felt slight palpitation of the heart in 35 minutes, and in 90 minutes his vision and hearing were distinctly affected. and he felt staggery, with abnormal panting on running up and down stairs. In two hours his vision and hearing were markedly impaired, and there was some confusion of mind, with throbbing headache. He concluded from his experiment that a content of 0.2 per cent of CO is very dangerous to man.

Koren showed in 1891 that progressive pernicious anemia is one of the symptoms of CO poisoning, and described the following pathological effects·

Dilatation of the heart, enlargement of the spleen, considerable decrease in the number of red blood corpuscles, and peptornuria. Postmortem of a fatal case showed that all the internal organs exhibited great pallor; the heart musculature was thickened; the heart was microscopically yellow dotted and showed advanced fatty degeneration; spleen was considerably enlarged and of hard consistency.

Mott made a postmortem examination in the case of a woman found unconscious from illuminating gas poisoning and who died four days later without regaining consciousness. He said that he never saw such extensive and general capillary hemorrhage in the brain as in this case.

Pulvertaft reported a case of spontaneous rupture of the heart in a youth of 19 due to carbon monoxide poisoning.

Lewin found that CO destroyed brain function of a dog so it did not know its master. He stated that in cases of CO poisoning, there is formed sooner or later in the brain great material changes of deterioration.

Symptoms of paralysis and other nerve affections present in cases of carbon monoxide poisoning, show the specific effect of the poisons on the brain and other nerve centers. For this reason CO is referred to as a brain poison.

In February, 1945 Chief Justice Edward C. Eicher of the U.S. District Court, "died in his sleep at his home in Alexandria, Virginia. He was 65." The basic cause of death was polluted air.

December 5th, 1944, Roger Bresnahan, considered by many as one of the greatest major league catchers of all-time, died at his home in Toledo, of "a heart attack." He was 64. Basic cause of death, polluted air.

Wendell Willkie, republican candidate for President in 1940, died in December, 1944, in his sleep at a certain hospital. "His wife, standing 'by his bedside, looked down into his still boyish face as his life flickered out." Basic cause of death, polluted air.

Cerebral hemorrhage caused the death of General Edwin M. Watson on February 27th, 1945, age 61. He was the late President Roosevelt's military aide and made his official appointments. Basic cause of death, polluted air.

In April, 1945, President F. D. Roosevelt died suddenly of cerebral hemorrhage; age 63. Basic cause of death, polluted air.

On March 13th, 1943, J. P. Morgan, the New York banker "who made his banking firm a colossus of the financial world and his very name a symbol of extreme wealth and power," died of "a heart ailment." Basic cause of death, polluted air.

Startling evidence that carbon monoxide gas is a "brain poison," appears in the fact that, according to the press of November 28th, 1947, psychiatrists estimate that 1 in 16 in the U.S.A. is weak mentally. The report says that Dr.

Valdimir Eliasberg stated that there are 800,-
000 insane people in various institiutions, and
eight million more are wandering thru the
cities, because families and friends consider
•them harmless eccentrics and let it go at that.
Millions more are in the beginning stages of
paresis.

The press of October 13th, 1947, carried
an item headed "Insanity More Prevalent in
City," which said:

> "The nearer you live to the center of a large
> city, the more likely you are to go insane. These
> are the conclusions of a study of the geography of
> insanity in five large cities of the USA.

> "Psychiatrists have long known that city people
> go crazy more often than country people do, but the
> discovery of well-defined insanity zones within cities
> surprised even them. The rate of lunacy lessens as
> you travel from the center of a city."

There is no mystery nor superstition surrounding the subject. The facts are clear and
comprehensive. Where the air in the center of
cities is more heavily charged with CO from
motor cars, tobacco smoke, coal smoke, and
other sources, there occurs the highest incidence
of insanity.   •

As we approach the periphery of the cities,
with less CO in the air, there is less insanity.
When we reach the better air of the open country, the incidence of insanity diminishes still
more, and perhaps would disappear completely

if country folks never visited the cities, and if their own homes were not frequently filled with tobacco smoke.

We have mentioned some of the Symptoms of Carbon Monoxide poisoning. This is all new to you. For the doctors call these conditions "symptoms of disease." There is no disease.

According to the doctor, the patient is suffering from the "attack" of some disease, and gives it a name after studying the "symptoms." Then he prescribes some remedy according to the teachings of his school.

Consider the preposterous medical claims regarding "symptomology and diagnosis" — the "most important branches of general pathology." "General pathology" amounts to less than a cup of cold water.

Also consider the ridiculous medical claims of "war against disease," that germs are the cause of "disease," that by the use of vaccines and serums, filthy poisons, medical art will "stamp out disease." There is no disease.

As you reflect on these false medical theories and practices, fix in your mind the fact that "medical art" is one of the biggest frauds on earth, and so proclaimed thru the ages by the leading doctors of the world.

Remember these symptoms of carbon monoxide poisoning, and keep the fact in mind that

the list given is far from complete. For out
of these symptoms more symptoms grow.

"Air is the Life of God," says one writer. "All
Breath is of God and in God," says another, who
adds:

"With every breath (and in no other way) you
are linked with the Divine.

"The mystery of Life itself, of all that is, may
be discovered by watching the Breath of Life breathing itself within you, according to the ancient seers
and sages."

Still humanity fears Air because of the teaching of medical schools.

"Don't let a draft of air strike you," warns
the doctor who knows only what his school
has taught him, and who dies of the same ailments and at the same age as his patients who
seek his help.

An intelligent person would observe these
things and shun the doctors. You show me
one person with good-old-common-horse-sense,
and I'll show you ten million halfwits and nit-
wits.

"All Life comes right out of the Air," writes
a distinguished author. Whence cometh Electricity? Whence cometh the mysterious power
that makes your radio function?

"There are wonders in the Air you breathe
that no man can ever explain," says a noted
writer.

Man became a Living Soul when into his Nostrils the Creative Power breathed the Breath of Life, say the Ancient Masters.

You breathe to live; to fill the body with strength and energy, vigor and vitality. You think these come from food. You seek them in tonics and vitamins. You are mistaken and a victim of commercialism.

AIR IS-LIFE

The Breath of Life makes man a Living Soul. But you doubt it. You think food makes you live and gives you energy. The medical schools so teach.

A soldier, "fighting for freedom" on the European front, during the last war, had his throat cut by a sharp fragment of steel from a bomb, and fell in a heap as though shot thru the heart.

His buddy rushed to his side. An examination showed no injury except a slight cut in the windpipe, just below the larynx (Adam's apple). This allowed the windpipe to close so air could not enter the lungs.

Quickly the man slipped his fountain pen into the trachea (wind pipe) to hold it open so air could enter; and, presto, the man immediately rose to his feet and walked as though nothing had happened.

Walking jarred the pen out and it fell to the ground—and so did the soldier. He could not move and appeared dead. He was dead. Even his heart stopped beating.

Quickly the pen was again inserted into the trachea to hold it open so air could enter the lungs, and again the dead man came back to life, rose to his feet and walked.

Here is absolute proof that Life comes out of the air you breathe. When you stop breathing you stop living. You will never die as long as you breathe, unless the air you breathe is polluted. And polluted air is the deadly agent we shall mention more fully.

This time the man held the pen in place with his hand until he reached a first-aid station, where a surgeon repaired the injury, which soon healed and the soldier's life was saved.

As steam moves the wheels of the locomotive so Air moves the Wheels of Life.

Fuel in the firebox of the locomotive is useless unless there is water and steam in the boiler.

Food in the food-box of man is useless unless there is Air in his lungs. If that air is badly polluted, it can destroy health and life quicker than anything else.

FOOD

You worry about what you eat while giving no thought to what you breathe. It is a mistake and you receive the consequences.

Ten years ago a case was reported in the newspapers of a woman in St. Paul, Minn., who did not eat for seven years. She was Mrs. Martha Nasch.

For commercial reasons such information is quickly smothered, and we were never able to get a definite report on the matter.

A similar case was reported in Spain that came under medical observation. This woman had taken nothing to eat or drink for fifteen years.

Other instances of persons not eating for long periods of time have been reported.

The press reported the case of Kakudo Yamashita, a cemetery caretaker of Tokyo, who lived for 35 years on nothing but uncooked tree leaves, weeds and grass. He was then 80 years old and said to be in excellent health.

In the press of January 25th, 1938, Ripley reported the case of Giovanni Succi who publicly fasted 80 periods of 30 days and 20 periods of 40 days, a total of 3200 days without food in 10 years. As there are 3,650 days in 10 years, Succi went without eating eight years and 280 days in ten years.

Where is the food racketeer who says a man is what he eats? Where is the doctor who says you must eat plenty to keep up your strength. He knows nothing of the Breath of Life.

Medical schools are ruled by commercialism. If they were ruled by a desire to help humanity, as they claim, then they would learn, to the detriment of commercialism, that FOOD is NOT the source of vigor and vitality.

TRUTH is easily found by those who sincerely and intelligently search for it. But intelligence is a mighty scarce quality.

THE MYTH OF NUTRITION

The spread of knowledge based on Truth is bad for racketeers. Today we hear on the radio and read in newspapers and magazines so much about calories and body requirements in vitamins, etc. All this goes well with the theory of eating as much as possible to nourish the body. But what FALSE teaching this is as you will find out by reading THE NUTRITIONAL MYTH, obtainable from the publishers of this book.

An account recently appeared in a certain magazine to the effect that one Oswald Beard, a veteran of World War I, was wounded in the stomach, and for the last ten years he has subsisted entirely on nothing more substantial than tea, spiked with plenty of cream and sugar. He drinks about sixty cups a day. His home is at St. Anne's on Sea, England.

Obviously Mr. Beard could have chosen a much better liquid to drink but he didn't and according to dietetic people he should have been dead long ago because his diet is inadequate. Wonder how they would explain the way Mr. Beard gets his nourishment?

The Ancient Masters held that the essential function of food in the adult was to transmit electrical energy to activate atomic activity in the organism.

They claimed to be able to accomplish the same results thru their special breathing exercises, especially in an environment where the air is exceedingly pure and highly electrified, as it is in the ozonated air of higher altitudes. That is the secret reason why they dwelt in the highlands and mountains.

OZONATED AIR

OZONE: An allotropic modification of Oxygen, occuring after the passage of electricity thru the air. Its molecules are believed to contain three atoms of oxygen.—Dict.

For several years a few scientists have been delving into the virtues of a cosmic ether called Ozone.

There is little information on the subject. Some believe Ozone is a filter for the sun's rays as they descend to the earth. Others think it is Oxygen to which another link has been added. For that reason it is referred to as O/3.

Scientists agree that Ozone is a peculiar substance. It is used for bleaching, as a powerful disinfectant, and as a means of purifying water. Recently it has been blended with highly distilled oils and used with some success in the treatment of respiratory ailments.

Ozone has a characteristic odor. It is claimed to be 1/5 as heavy as $O/2$, yet it resembles ordinary Oxygen in its chemical content, although it registers a great degree of activity. Until recently it presented an almost insurmountable problem of screening out the poisonous nitrogen oxides.

Ozone has been found to increase the oxyhemoglobin content of the blood. This means an extra amount of oxygenated hemoglobin in the corpuscles of the arterial blood. It means more of that which the body needs.

One of the largest ozonating systems in use is in the Central London Railway. It is recorded that during a severe influenza epidemic, motor drivers who ran thru the tubes daily were free of the disorder.

In a small way Ozone is being used in hospitals, public schools and in the sterilization of water systems. The fact remains that it is still in embryonic stages of development. The average person has never heard of it except as an element present in the air after an electric storm, or in connection with the mountains or seashore.

In modern times people are so ignorant that they hardly know why they breathe, and dis- regard entirely the quality of the air they breathe.

The Ancient Masters were well-versed in these matters and taught them to their follow- ers. They termed Pure Air the Breath of Life and developed a system of special breathing exercises.

They taught men to inhale thru the nose, but to exhale thru the mouth. As they sent forth the foul air of the lungs, they puckered up the lips, as though blowing out a candle several feet away. This forced the Black Breath of Death and its poisonous content away from their body and entirely beyond their aura. which extends outward from the surface of all parts of the body for a distance of about 18 inches.

At each exhalation the lungs eliminate enough toxic matter to poison a barrel-full of air. Each person in a room needs 3,000 cubic feet of fresh air per hour.

This means that the hermit's hut in the hills will soon be filled with polluted air, unless doors and windows are kept open at all times.

There is not a home in the north in winter that it not saturated with polluted air because the killing cold makes ventilation impossible.

SOURCE OF ENERGY

What is Energy? What is Vital Force? What is Nerve Force? Ask the doctor and observe his sneering smile to hide his ignorance as he attempts a long medical explanation which means nothing.

Luke refers to Jesus, when he was only 12 years old, as sitting in the midst of the doctors in the temple, both hearing them, and asking them questions; and all that heard him were astonished at his understanding and answers. (Luke 2:42-47).

Nothing strange about that. The same can be done today by any child of 12 that has been properly instructed for 30 days in the Mysteries of Life, which the doctors are not. They are even taught that there is no such entity as the Life Principle.

Medical schools claim that Food is the source of vital energy.

You are a child of 12 and want to prove that medical schools are wrong. Make this test:

1. Fast for five days in the country where the air is pure and see your health improve Notice whether you lose your energy.

2. Fill your stomach with food and stop breathing for five minutes and see what happens. Notice what becomes of your energy.

3. Fill your stomach with food, go into your garage and start the motor of your car and close doors and windows. Notice how soon you lose all energy and faint and fall.

Tell this to the doctor as proof the Food is not the source of vital energy, and see him smile -and pity your ignorance.

Electricity is energy and comes out of the air. That fact is common knowledge. Even the medical schools endorse that view.

Why doubt that Life, a form of vitality of the highest type, comes out of the Air?

Back to the Ancient Masters we must always go to acquire facts about the Life Principle, which Jesus said quickens (animates) the flesh (Jn. 6:63). They taught knowledge based on Truth because they were FREE from the control of commercialism.

They contended and proved that it was possible, in those days, for man to live without eating, provided he practiced certain breathing exercises and dwelt in an environment where the air is pure and highly electrified, as it is in the ozonated air of higher altitudes far removed from the poisonous fumes of industrialism.

But that was in the days when man's lung
capacity was much greater than now. Since
then the Breathing Organs of man have decreased in size and degenerated in function.
Even now his lungs are so large that they inhale
and digest daily approximately 777,000 cubic
inches of air, and in the same time purify 125
barrels of blood.

The Ancient Masters taught that the Living
Organism is not comparable to any man-made-
machine.

The Living Organism is not similar to a
steam engine that requires a constant fuel supply to keep it working. It is more of the nature of an Electrical Apparatus, and is continually recharged and vitalized by a Mysterious
Energy which comes out of the Air and about
which modern science knows nothing.

Knowing the secrets of Nature, these Ancient
Masters dwelt in the ozonated air of high regions. Such air is not only exceptionally pure,
but contains Oxygen charged with Ozone. If
we but knew all the secrets we would then
understand why they lived hundreds of years.

When man inhales Pure Air highly charged
with Ozone, the electrical rechargement and
vitalization of the body is increased, and in the
same ratio the desire and need for food decrease.
That is why commercialism profits by keeping
man in ignorance.

CONTACT WITH GOD

It is the Holy Spirit that quickens and animates the flesh. (Gen. 2:7: Eccl. 12:7; John 4;24; 6:63).

Therefore, marvel not that we say unto you, "With every Breath ye are linked directly with the Divine." For Truth is always stranger than fiction. Yet you refuse to believe.

It has ever been thus. Man has always rejected truth and embraced error. Jesus said unto the ignorant skeptics—

"If they hear not Moses and the prophets, neither will they be persuaded (to believe Truth), though one rose from the dead. (Luke 16:31).

Man's body is energized because he is a Living Soul, and he is a Living Soul by reason of the fact that the Divine Breath (Essence) of Life is in his nostrils, in his lungs, in his nerves, in his blood, in his brain, in his flesh. (Job 27:3).

The Ancient Masters repeat this fact over and over again; yet ye believe them not. The fool says Food is the Source of Energy.

The Ancient Masters knew there is one definite avenue of physical contact with God, and only one. That is thru the Air Organs of the body.

From the Creative Source there constantly and silently flows the Essence of Life. It enters the body thru the Air Organs; and when you stop breathing you stop living.

Now you know why your Lungs are by far the largest and most vital organs of your body. Yet the so-called scientists attach no special significance either to their size or their function, and they drop dead of heart disease from inhaling polluted air just as the dumb laymen do.

Instead of living as you perhaps do in a rotten environment of polluted air, you should flee to a region of the best air you can find. For thru your Air Organs you are in direct physical and spiritual contact with the Creative Spirit, call it God if you please.

You doubt it because of ignorance, yet with every breath you are linked with the Divine. But you know it not because teaching the multitude the Truth yields no profit.

Man is in the quagmire of despair because a cleverly prepared program of misinformation prevents him from acquiring that knowledge which would make him Master of his Destiny.

Knowledge based on Truth is the only power that sets man free; and commercialism ridicules and discredits the teachers of Truth because Free Men would never support the enslaving conditions of civilization by which modern man is surrounded.

If medical schools or governments were interested in human betterment, they would send commissions to investigate the living conditions of those tribes in the tropics that are free of disease, such as the Bene tribe of Negroes in the Palm Belt of the Niger River in Africa, or the Wai Wai Indians of Brazek, reported to be free of all modern day ills.

But no one has a desire to kill a business that brings in more than five billion dollars a year. And the cross always awaits him who would interfere with that business by teaching Truth to the multitude.

WHAT YOU BREATHE

You are a Living Soul only because the Divine Breath of Life, directly from the Creative Source, flows into your body, blood, brain, thru your marvelous Air Organs, giving you strength, energy, Life.

Man is made to breathe Pure Air. What kind of air does he breathe?

You know little of the manner in which a rotten civilization, commercialism and industrialism have transformed the Pure Breath of Life into a stream of pollution that poisons you from birth till death with every breath you take.

That stream of polluted air sends your precious body down to an early grave by a definite process of gradual degeneration, the symptoms of which are called diseases by the doctors.

You do know a little about food; and false

teaching leads you to believe your strength and energy come from what you eat.

If you knew as much about the kind of Air you breathe as you do about the kind of food you eat, you would pack your trunk and move to a cleaner, more healthful environment before the Sun set.

Nashville, Tennessee is not considered a smoky city. According to a press report, a thirty day survey of its air showed that in 30 days, from January 15th to February 15th, 1938, more than 22,000 pounds of soot, per square mile, fell upon that center of civilization—more than 200 tons covering the whole municipality.

The Cincinnati Enquirer of December 9th, 1930, published data showing the amount of gas, fumes, soot, and dust in the air of that place. In the business section where observations were made at 4th and Vine Streets the total deposit of filth was 1,176.02 tons per square mile.

As to the condition of the air in Cleveland, the Press of November 13th, 1938, stated—

"Fifty thousand tons of soot float in the atmosphere of this city of a million—100 pounds for every inhabitant . . . One of the dirtiest sections produced 87.15 tons of grime in insoluble solids, such as carbons, fly ash, and ferrous oxide."

The account stated that while the air of New York City is bad there are 14 other cities where the air is worse, and listed them as follows:

1. St. Louis	10. Baltimore	19. Des Moines
2. Cincinnati	11. Milwaukee	20. Washington
3. Pittsburgh	12. Columbus	21. Denver
4. Detroit	13. Toledo	22. New Orleans
5. Chicago	14. Philadelphia	23. San
6. Indianapolis	15. N. Y. City	Francisco
7. Cleveland	16. Kansas City	24. Boston
8. Louisville	17. Los Angeles	
9. Buffalo	18. Minneapolis	

For years Pittsburgh was termed the "Smoky City," but now it has fallen to third place.

Los Angeles has so many industrial plants pouring out smoke and soot that the city and surrounding country are shrouded in it. The mountains, only 35 miles away, can be seen only occasionally during winter shortly after the air has been somewhat cleansed by rainfall.

The press of October 13th, 1937, stated that Los Angeles stood first among the larger cities of the U.S. in tuberculosis mortality in 1936, with a rate of 87 deaths per 100,000 population.

This is an example of what civilization, commercialism and industrialism are doing to those regions of the earth where they have gained a foothold.

According to a study made by the Temperature Research Foundation of the Kelvinator Corporation, there is precipitated in the lungs

of the average person within the short space
of one year, more than 1.2 pounds of filth
from the air.   The Report said:—

"The average filth-fall in a large city is approximately 230 tons per square mile per
month, according to the study."

The New York World-Telegram of February 6th, 1937, stated that a count of dirt
particles caught by the air-washing systems in
New York motion-picture theaters showed,
that for 88,200,000 cubic feet of air taken in
by the air-conditioning system, there is 15 cubic
feet of dirt, which means that a layer of air
over New York 200 feet high, contains 1,780
tons of dust, soot and filth.

When we know the kind of an environment
into which children are born, it is easily understood why many of them die while yet young
of ailments resulting from the polluted air they
breathe.

Dr. Duncan S. Johnson, director of the bo-
tanical garden at Johns Hopkins University.
Baltimore, was quoted in the press of December 24th, 1930 at stating that— .

"Eventual death of all plant-life in America's
big cities was predicted unless smoke and exhaust fumes are curbed."

Dr. C. W. Dowden of Louisville was quoted
in the New York Times of July 13th, 1929,
as asserting that—

"Residents in big cities, as a result of the increase in the number of motor cars, are facing a growing menace to health from the deadly carbon-monoxide saturation of the atmosphere."

U.S. Authorities have demonstrated a concentration of 0.62 parts of carbon monoxide per 10,000 cubic centimeters of air at street level in busy sections of cities of 500,000 population or over.

In 1926 Drs. Wilson, Gates, Owen and Sawson reported blood tests made of 14 policemen, after eight hours on traffic duty in Philadelphia, and they showed an absorption of carbon monoxide of between 20 and 30 per cent of saturation.

A concentration only two parts in ten thousand will produce the symptoms of headache, mental dullness, muscular fatigue and loss of energy in a few hours. These symptoms in city workers and city dwellers are common and usually disregarded. The victims look to foods and vitamins for relief, not knowing the cause of the trouble.

Scientists of the Harvard Laboratories, risking their lives to discover more about carbon monoxide gas, found the average man can endure it only until his blood is one-third saturated.

Scientists agree that city air is a polluted mixture of industrial fumes, such as carbon monoxide, sulphuric acid, hydrochloric acid, nitric acid, hydrocyanic acid, benzene, methane, sulphur, and other dangerous chemicals too numerous to mention.

In addition to these poisonous industrial fumes, city air is saturated with exhaust gas from motor cars and trucks. This deadly gas consists of carbon-monoxide, carbon-dioxide, lead-oxide, lead carbonates, free gasoline, and complicated benzine chain compounds of the hydrocarbon series.

These substances are deadly poisonous to man. Only a few grains of hydrocyanic acid produces violent death quickly.

This is the kind of air you breathe in the cities from birth till death, and these poisons are competent to cause any disorder, from colds to cancer.

Professor H. Landsburg, Geophysical Laboratory, Pennsylvania State college, writes—

"Wherever human dwellings are, wherever industry has found a foothold, these numbers of dust particles in the air are vastly increased, and many substances of high chemical activity are added to the list.

"Among the more dangerous compounds, nitric acid and sulphuric acid are always present in combustion gases. It thus results that in our cities an average of 2,500,000 particles per cubic inch are present."

The fumes of sulphuric acid are heavier than air. They hang like a death pall over large areas where used by industries. They are so corrosive that in certain sections the fumes eat up clothing hung on wash lines. Sulphuric acid eats ulcers in the skin. It eats slowly like a cancer into those victims who breathe it.

LUNG DEGENERATION

The lungs of man, as a result of breathing the polluted air of civilization, are consumed by the corrosive action of these poisons, which gnaw away at his lungs as they do at clothing hung out to dry.

Lung degeneration is common in the nation because polluted air is so prevalent. Dr. Thomas Darlington, former health commissioner of New York City, says:—

"The products of combustion also irritate the eyes, ears, nose, throat, the respiratory tract, the bronchial tubes, and the gastro-intestinal areas.

"In the lungs the carbon particles accumulate and become imbedded in the air cells, and in time the lungs change from natural pink to black.

"I have performed many autopsies upon New Yorkers, and almost without exception their lungs were as black as night.

"I could present an impressive list of diseases in which the influence of polluted air is known.

"It is in pneumonia, of the acute disorders, that the influence of polluted air falls most disastrously.

"Pneumonia ranks first; in the industrial U.S., in the list of acute diseases as a cause of death. It takes away vigorous adults in the most useful years of their lives.

"There is a striking parallel between smokiness of cities and higher pneumonia mortality. The soot having coated the interior of the lungs, it obstructs their natural eliminative processes, which are essential for victory in a patient's fight against pneumonia." (Quoted by W. B. Courtney under title "Our Smoky Cities," in Collier's).

Another investigator asserts that the lungs of any person living in a large city for five years becomes as black as soot from the carbon that coats the interior of the lungs. Recovery from this condition is impossible, and early death is certain for the victim. If he suddenly drops dead or dies in his sleep, the doctor says, "Heart disease."

No one living in the cities is free of this condition, because the cities are enveloped in a haze of polluted air.

The doctors, nurses, city health authorities —all of them have black lungs undergoing a process of degeneration, the same as their patients.

The doctors drop dead just as their patients do. Read the accounts in the daily press.

Here you are—"Dr. C. E. Ryan, 69, died of a heart attack as he was delivering a baby. Others stepped in to complete his duties, and mother and child are doing well." (Press of June 4, 1944).

Another doctor, at the bedside of his patient, drops dead of "heart disease."

But it's not heart disease. The cause is polluted air. The body can stand just so much, then it goes down.

How can a person live long when his lungs are as black as soot from a coating of carbon on their interior walls? That is the condition of the lungs of every person who has lived five years in a large city.

Sometimes city air is so polluted that people are struck down while on the streets or at work. In June, 1944, more than 500 persons were felled to the sidewalk by polluted air at a busy intersection in Brooklyn.

City air is so saturated with foul fumes at all times, that just a little more added is all that is needed to send city dwellers on to the grave.

See them going. Dropping dead of "heart disease." Hospitals filled to the roof and more being built. Doctors' offices, crowded with the victims who live in the death-traps called cities.

When the air man breathes is just slightly polluted, it causes only slight sickness, as colds, coughs, hay fever. This continues thru the years and the result is some chronic malady— then death.

When the air pollution is greater, the sickness is more severe, as influenza, pneumonia, asthma.

Death comes when air pollution is so great that it paralyzes the nerves of the brain, lungs, and heart. Then we have cases of cerebral hemorrhage, as in the case of President Roosevelt, or "heart failure," which today is taking people at an alarming rate.

From birth till death the body passes thru a steady process of degeneration which results from constantly breathing the polluted air of civilization.

The early disorders appear in the nose, throat and lungs—in the Air Organs.

GOOD LUNGS

Good lungs are found only in the realm of pure air, and pure air is found only in regions far removed from industrialism, commercialism and "modern homes."

Early in 1934 some sincere health seekers went to Panama to live more in harmony with the law of life and enjoy the blessings of health One was Dr. Jacob Goldwasser, who wrote me on January 14th, 1945, stating—

> "In regard to Pure Air. I made a circle back of my house 124 feet in circumference. This morning I ran five miles around this circle in 45 minutes at a trot. Not fast running. I have already done 10 miles.

"The amazing thing is, that I don't have to open my mouth in these runs for second wind.

"In contrast, when I first came here from New York City I puffed and puffed with open mouth for a mile run.

"In the dry season I go to town on foot for mail, some 18 or 20 miles round trip, once or twice a week.

"The sun comes out at 7 a.m. and I hoof into town without water or food. On returning, the walk is mostly uphill and hotter towards noon. I passed sparkling streams, yet don't touch water until 5 p.m.

"This is my weekly fast day, where I stop eating and drinking at 5 p.m. on Thursday until 5 p.m. the next day. Then my wife prepares a pitcher of six glasses of orange juice mixed with a little raw sugar cane sap which we drink. When darkness comes we go to bed.

"We came to the tropics for health, and it is a serious business with us. We look forward to an age of 150 years if we are wise enough to stay in the tropics for the rest of our days."

Behold this man and wife living in harmony with God's Plan of Life as described in 2nd chapter of Genesis.

See the vast improvement in his lungs since leaving the polluted air of New York and living eleven years in the tropics.

His lungs are now in such excellent shape that they easily supply the requisite amount of oxygen for his body's needs without opening his mouth while running.

See how far you can run without opening your mouth for more air. Your lung capacity is your energy and vital capacity. Pure Air keeps your lungs in good shape while polluted air ruins them. When you stop breathing you stop living.

You are on the wrong track when you look to food and vitamins for energy and vitality.

When you feel tired and ache all over from head to heels, do you know the cause of it? The cause is breathing polluted air, and the only remedy is pure air.

That simple knowledge of priceless value will never get to the multitude as long as pro- fitmongers can keep it concealed.

The day when you begin to breathe pure air will be the day when your health will begin to improve.

THE COMMON COLD

Writing in Nature's Path on the subject of Colds, Dr. A. L. Allen says: "The most prev- alent and most mysterious disease troubling humanity and confusing the medical profession today is the Common Cold." (P. 203).

The common cold is the most prevalent "disease" because civilization lives and labors in a cloud of polluted air, and polluted air is the cause of colds.

The common cold is the most mysterious disease because medical schools have not found the underlying cause of colds.

If you could read Nature's warning signals, that common cold would tell you a strange story. But years of miseducation have dynamited the natural instinct out of man, and filled his head with nonsense.

The common cold is the first signal of Nature to warn you that your Environment is unfit for human occupation.

The common cold is the first warning that you are starting down the broad road of degeneration that leads to the grave.

Nose, throat and lung ailments are common, because polluted air is common. Doctors know not the cause of these because medical schools are sordid institutions of profit and not interested in human betterment.

DEGENERATION PROGRESSES

To you a baby is born and you are happy. You begin to plan its future and want to see it grow into a fine man or woman.

The environment in which the child is born is one of polluted air, and that air begins to eat

away at the child's lungs before it is ten days
old.

Follow the trail of this degenerative process
from the birth of the child, and learn where
that process begins and why.

Here are the facts, and they are hard to face.
Vital statistics show that the chief cause of
death in children from birth up to the age of 9
years, is disorders of the Breathing Organs.

Breathing polluted air causes a process of
degeneration in the lungs of children that moves
so rapidly, that by the time a child is four or
five years old, that process of degeneration has
gone so far that it can be revealed by an x-ray
examination, which shows tiny white spots in
the lungs.

That information may shock you, but it is
true.

What do the doctors say about these small
white spots in the lungs?   They term them
"small stone coffins in which are buried the
germ of tuberculosis."   What fools.

The facts are, those white spots are ruptured air cells that have healed.

But no longer can they function as air cells.
They are done. Their function is forever lost.

They are now "small stone coffins" in which
are buried the worthless remains of precious

air cells which once formed the connecting link with the Creative Source by inhaling and digesting the Divine Breath of Life, and passing it, with its cargo of vital 'energy, on to the blood, the nerves, and the brain, but which cells are now as useless as a withered and paralyzed arm.

Little do you know of the damage done to your lungs when you inhale polluted air. When the air is sufficiently foul, the lung cells grow inflamed and swollen, producing a tight feeling in the chest. Some of the cells rupture, burst. Then their function is forever gone.

When the larger cells burst, then the victim coughs up blood that seeps from the tiny blood vessels into the air cavity of the lungs. Behold how your lungs degenerate, and why.

The tiny vessels heal in time, and you think you have recovered. So does the doctor.

NO COMPLETE RECOVERY

Each illness is a step down the ladder to the grave. If the illness is slight, that downward step is short. If the illness is severe, that downward step is longer.

All recoveries from each illness are only partial. Of course the victim does not notice it at first. But the day comes when it is painfully noticeable.

Each illness is an indication that you are go-
down the ladder of degeneration.   And there
is no return. You go down, down, down; but
you never go up again.   You never return to
that point where you were prior to your first
illness. Each subsequent illness takes you farther down.

It may be only a cold, but it tells the same
story. The polluted air of your environment
is doing its deadly work and dragging you
down.

Then comes that day when you have pneumonia or a serious case of influenza.   You may
not die, but you will experience a definite degree of weakness that will always remain to
make you realize that you are going down.
Doctors call it the work of old age.

We receive letters from the victims who tell
us they seem unable to get their strength back,
no matter what they eat.

How can we ever make these people understand?

Understand this: A cut finger heals.   But
the repaired spot is composed of low grade,
scar tissue, which never functions 100 per cent
as the original tissue did.

It's the same with ruptured air cells in the
lungs.   They heal, but something terrible has
happened. It is like a severed finger which you

can never use again. The respiratory function of those tiny lung cells is gone for good.

Just that much is your lung capacity decreased. That goes on from year to year because you breathe polluted air from year to year.

As your lung capacity decreases, so your vitality also decreases. You see your energy fading. You begin to slow up, to get wobbly on your feet, and your strength decreases.

Why? You eat the same as ever. You are just growing old says the doctor. It is more difficult to explain why man dies, says science, that to explain why he should live forever. Dr. Munroe stated:

"The human frame as a machine is perfect. It contains within itself no marks by which we can possibly predict its decay. It is apparently intended to go on forever." (The Divine Life, p. 101).

We are explaining why man fails to live forever. He guides his own destiny and receives what he deserves. (Gal. 6:7).

Bad climate, bad environment, and bad habits set into operation the process of degeneration.

Each illness thru life springs from the process of degeneration. The work of the degenerative process is what medical schools term the body's wearing out.

But the body can't wear out, it does not wear out, and no part of it can wear out. Listen to the words of Dr. J. C. Dalton, professor of physiology, College of Physicians and Surgeons, New York.

> "A continuous change goes on in the substance of the organs of the entire body, by which their parts and materials are constantly decomposed and constantly renewed.
>
> "Throughout the whole frame of the body, Nature is incessantly engaged in taking apart the tissues of which the body is composed, and in building them over again of new, fresh materials; so that the tissues of the body are accordingly always renewed and always ready to perform their allotted work." (Physiology #505).

Such body can't wear out; it can't grow old. How can it grow old when all of its cells and tissues are constantly being renewed from day to day and year to year?

OLD AGE

Old Age is a state of the body, not the period of its existence. It is a condition of decrepitude, and that condition does not depend upon the rotation of the earth, nor upon the rising and setting of the sun.

There is no such thing as a disease of Old Age. People never die of Old Age.

Dr. Howard T. Krasner, director of the Institute of Pathology, Western Reserve University of Cleveland, searched thru the records of 19,000 persons whose bodies had been carefully examined after death, and in not one case had the doctors written down "old age" as the cause of death. Every patient had died of some ailment that had nothing to do with his age.

This is what Dr. Krasner discovered in his investigation: Examining a so-called worn-out heart or blood-vessel revealed the fact that previous illnesses left inflamed areas and other marks of damage to the internal organs.

Dr. Krasner's investigation disclosed the fact that there is no such thing as complete recovery from illness.

Dr. Alexis Carrel mentions the matter in these words:

"Each thought, each action, each illness, has definitive consequences, inasmuch as we never separate ourselves from our past. We may apparently recover from a disease, or from a wrong deed. But the scar of those events we bear forever." (Man The Unknown, p. 170).

Each illness leaves you a little weaker. At first the weakness is too slight to be noticed. But the time does come when these things can be painfully noticed.

You remember how long it took you to recover from that last case of "flu." It left you with no energy. You, had no desire any more to run, or even walk fast.

Your friends told you that you were getting old. It is the work of old age, and must be expected. There you are. Ignorance again.

Life cannot wear out. The body cannot wear out. Why does a person appear to grow old? The answer is: Degeneration!

What is the cause? The answer is (1) Bad Climate, (2) Bad environment, (3) Bad habits.

There is no disease. There is no cure for what the doctors call disease. But there is a remedy which is: (1) Good Climate, (2) Good environment, (3) Good habits.

God's Plan of Life leaves no place for the doctor. That is why medical schools have no desire to learn anything about the Life Principle and its Law of Operation.

The doctors can live and thrive on human misery as long as the multitude can be kept in ignorance. One way to promote ignorance is to deceive the people and crush all sources of enlightment.

LOSING CONTACT WITH GOD

When your lungs begin to degenerate, it affects the whole body. So slight at first as not to be noticed, but by the time the average person reaches 40 he begins to break fast. He thinks it is the world of old age.

When you begin to weaken, the basic cause is Polluted Air. Every organ and gland begins to weaken. Then the doctors say, Be Careful, you are getting old, your body is wearing out, your heart is getting weak.

The body does not wear out. It is never more than seven years old. In every seven years the body is completely rebuilt and renewed, from the softest tissue to the hardest bone.

The physical body dies when it can no longer contact the Eternal Source of Life.

The polluted air in which you are born, and live, and labor, begins to degenerate your body in infancy.

Evidence of early degeneration appears in the form of disorders which the doctors term "children's diseases." There is no disease.

As the years pass you grow weaker in your ailments because of the progress of the degenerative process.

What is the remedy? There are no remedies, no cures. Know the Truth and let it set you free.

Physical death comes when physical contact with the Source of Life is entirely lost. That condition comes when lung degeneration has progressed so far that the lungs are no longer

able to inhale, digest and feed the Breath of
Life into the organism in sufficient quantities to
meet its needs.

POLLUTED AIR

Airplane pilots tell us that the umbrella of
black smoke, soot, grime, dirt, dust and filth
floating above the larger cities of the nation
have a spread of 200 miles or more.

Coming from the west, the blue haze becomes noticeable in the air 200 miles from Kansas City; and the blue haze extends unbroken
clear to the Atlantic coast.

There is no pure air from the Atlantic coast
of Boston way out to the wheat fields of western Kansas.

A man from Washington, D. C. visited us
in Florida, and his first words were: "How
clear the air is here. One can see for miles in
every direction."

Some years ago I made a trip to Cincinnati
and saw the blue haze in the air 200 miles before I reached St. Louis. I was in that blue haze
until I was 200 miles beyond St. Louis on my
return journey.

You will never die, barring accidents, until
your lungs have degenerated to a point where
they are no longer able to breathe into your
body enough of the Breath of Life to keep you
alive.

Lung degeneration results from (1) polluted air and (2) improper breathing.

If the air you breathe is polluted, breathing exercises are not only useless but injurious.

WHY MAN DIES.

We locked up in an iron safe a man in good health and left him there for 60 minutes. Then the safe was opened and the man was dead. Why did he die?

We put some healthy fish in a tub of water. In less than an hour the fish begin to come to the top of the water and gasp for breath, and will soon die unless the water is changed.

If the iron safe were equipped with a glass window so the man inside could be watched, it would be observed that he was gasping for breath before his demise.

Science terms this, Death by suffocation.

SUFFOCATION: The act of choking or stifling: a stopping of respiration, either by intercepting the passage of air to and from the lungs, or by inhaling smoke, dust, or air that is not respirable. (Webster's Dict., p. 1662).

On June 1st, 1944, more than 500 persons fell as though shot at a busy intersection in Brooklyn.

The cause: Poison gas leaking from a tank being transported in a truck to a Brooklyn pier.

The people began to cough, vomit, stagger.
and then fell flat, creating a scene resembling
war pictures.

Close the doors and windows of your garage, start the motor of your car, and see how
long you live. The deadly fumes of the exhaust will soon make you faint and fall, and
your end will come quickly.

The fish in the tub and the man in the safe
die from a deficiency of oxygen, according to
science.

Thru the act of breathing, the fish in the tub
and the man in the safe consume the available
supply of oxygen, then begin to gasp for breath
and perish.

But a deficiency of oxygen was not the cause
of death in the case of the man in the closed garage. There was plenty of oxygen in the air, but
the air was filled with the deadly fumes of the
exhaust.

Now we are getting down to the point: The
air you breathe in your home from year to year
is filled with foul fumes, not enough to cause
sudden death, but enough to create a toxic
condition of your blood and fill your body
with aches and pains.

You suffer from autointoxication, toxemia.
enervation, and in time these develop and grow,

from the same cause, into more serious conditions, which doctors term diseases and try to cure with their poisons.

Constantly breathing polluted air sets the process of degeneration into operation, and at last the body sinks down in a lifeless heap, to rise no more by its own power.

The foul fumes people breathe in their cities and homes have a serious effect on those tiny bodies which float in myriads in the blood, and are termed red corpuscles.

The red corpuscles have a double concave surface, and at their edges a perfectly smooth outline. The foul fumes in the air people inhale leads to rapid changes in these corpuscles. They lose their round shape, becoming oval and irregular; and instead of having a natural attraction for one another and running together, as they should do in good health, they lie loosely scattered before the eye, and indicate to a trained observer that the person from whose body they were taken, is physically depressed and seriously deficient in vigor and vitality.

Caged birds live a short life because of the polluted air they must breath in the buildings where they are kept.

People live a short life because of the polluted air they breathe in their homes and in the places where they labor.

The man in the safe died gasping for the Breath of Life.

When you die you will go gasping for the Breath of Life. Your end will be due to degeneration that resulted from inhaling foul air from the day you were born.

THE NEGLECTED SUBJECT

Teaching people to breathe pure air for health brings profit to no one, and receives no attention.

Read all the medical text books in the world and you will find nothing on polluted air. Read all the health literature of modern times and you will find little on polluted air.

We can cite doctors who have written libraries on health and disease, and not one has mentioned polluted air.

I have three courses by three different authors on the subject of Breathing, but not one of them mentions polluted air. One makes this absurd statement:

"What is meant by PURE air? By PURE air is meant air everywhere in the open." (p. 16).

What doctors and others write on health and disease is of little value if they fail to go back to fundamentals and consider the basic cause of human ailments in this civilization—POLLUTED AIR.

Health Science

PART 3.

The Universe is a Unit, being the effect of one cause. As the whole is composed of the parts, we are for this reason justified in assuming that the whole was produced as the parts are produced. It is inconceivable that there is one order of work for the whole, with a contrary order for the parts. And if the Universe is under the control of one Universal Law, all parts of it must be under control of the same law.

———————

The body, likewise, is a unit, and is the effect of one cause. Also, the whole is made up of the parts, and the whole was produced as the parts are produced. The same order of work that rules the whole, also rules the parts. Conversely, the same order of work that rules parts of the body, so small that they cannot be seen, is the same order that rules the whole.

Holding this fact before us as our guiding light, we shall proceed to state the primary cause of all disease, and explain the problem so clearly, that any one of common intelligence can easily understand it. Those accepting "as

their doctrines the precepts of men" (Matt.
15:9), may reject this truth because of its
sublime simplicity; but we as believers in the
Word of God, and not in the tradition of men,
should remember that the deepest truths ever
expounded have been the simplest and most
readily comprehended. There are no exceptions
in Nature; therefore the truth as to disease is no
exception to the rule of natural simplicity, regardless of all existing complexity and mystery,
invented by the greed of gold for its own base
ends, now surrounding disease.

The primary cause of disease is nothing more
or less than the (1) wrong use of things supplied by Nature—violation of the Law of God.
Since effect follows cause as night follows day,
we find the primary effect of the primary cause
to be (2) enervation (lowered vital resistance),
and toxemia (poison in the blood)—these being the first stages of all bodily disorders. Some
authors, who fail to go back to fundamentals
for their first principles, mistakes the primary
effect for the primary cause, and then divide
on the question, by one side holding that Toxemia is the primary cause; and the other, that
Enervation is.   As we shall see, both opinions
erroneous; for the primary cause of disease is
not found in the flesh.

It is strange that "science" should seek for
the cause of disease nowhere but within the

body, and for "cures" nowhere but without,
when the real situation is just the reverse. The
primary cause of disease is found without; and
the only "cure" in the Universe is the curative
power of and within the living organism. It
was just as sensible to search in the stone for
the cause that brings it back to earth, when
hurled into the air, or in the rain-drops for the
cause of their descent from the clouds, as to
search within the body for the cause of disease.
Certainly, the study of dead men, and of animals under vivisection, will never reveal the
cause of disease; for the cause is invisible, and
is not within the body. In fact, all causes are
invisible. Newton never saw the Power of
Gravitation. He learned of its existence thru
its effects. Effects only are all that we ever see.
Enervation-toxemia is merely the (2) primary
effect, while the (1) primary cause, as we have
stated, is (1) the violation of the Law of Life.

Having stated the (1) primary cause, and
the (2) primary effect, we next ask, What is
the (3) secondary cause? In a word, it is the
reaction of the body to the internal danger
(enervation-toxemia), produced by the (1)
violation of law. The violation of the Law of
Life invariably produces dangerous internal
conditions; and from such conditions the body
recoils by instinct, just as a man himself recoils
by nature from external danger. The instinc-
tive recoil arises from the spontaneous action of

the Great Invisible Force Within, which guides
and guards the living organism forever and
eternally.

We have now come to the (4) secondary
effect. Here lies the very crux of the whole matter.   Secondary effects have been treated as
demons and diseases since the birth of therapeutics. without any knowledge of their underlying and mystifying cause.   Today, legions of
learned men, termed "scientists," are earnestly
engaged in extensive research work, endeavor-
ing to solve the unknown cause of these secondary effects (disease), and learn how to treat,
"cure," and prevent them. Drugs, serums, and
knives have been and now are the agents used
in the attempt to drive these secondardy effects
from the body, and thus "cure" the "disease."
Vaccination and inoculation are practiced to
prevent these secondary effects from "attacking
healthy bodies." But all efforts have failed and
must continue to fail, because the theory is
wrong. Due to its vital importance, we shall
give the secondary effects by a concrete example.

A man meets an enemy. The man is healthy;
his body is normal. The enemy he subdues and
conquers after a most strenuous struggle, which
leaves him panting for breath, with violent
pulsation of the heart, covered with perspiration, without appetite and weak and exhausted.
The additional strength was supplied for the

struggle by a general acceleration of all the functions of the body to meet the emergency. The shock of the struggle may be so severe, and the man's strength so depleted, that he becomes unconscious soon after it ends, and is compelled by weakness and exhaustion to lie in bed for several days. However, he soon recovers his former state of health without "treatment" or "medicine" of any sort.

Here is the (4) secondary effect of the body's reaction to threatened danger. The quickening of the functions, being an abnormal state created to counteract an abnormal condition, is followed by a period of weakness and exhaustion, in accordance with the law that "action and reaction are equal, but opposite." We can correctly say that the man, hale, hearty, strong and vigorous when he met the enemy, is "diseased" ere the battle barely begins; for the abnormal functions (reactions) here noted, are similar indeed to those termed and treated as "disease."

We observe that the (4) secondary effect of the body's reaction to danger within, is similar to that of the body's reaction to danger without—rapid respiration, violent pulsation, profuse perspiration, and a general acceleration of all the functions. However, there is this difference: The danger within arises from an excess of toxins and foreign matter that are corrupting the body; and since the reaction has for its

sole purpose the elimination of the destructive
eternal elements, in the various symptom complexes of vomiting, diarrhoea, diphtheria, fevers, pneumonia, smallpox, and other so-called
acute diseases, we have and observe the surface
indications of this elimination.

As the body concentrates its vital forces for
the struggle against the internal danger, a feeling of weakness and fatigue may be noticed.
The blood may recede from the surface, and the
patient experience a "chill" as a result. When all
is in readiness, and not before, a vigorous reaction sets in. The heart begins a violent throbbing that sends the blood rushing in torrents
to all parts of the body, and consequently in-
creases the temperature.   .

The blood is the marvelous stream that turns
the wheels of life. As its flow quickens, there is
a spontaneous and a simultaneous quickening
of the function of all the organs. For the body,
as we have said, is a unit, and all parts, under
one law, work together, and in perfect harmony
with the whole. Therefore, the faster the blood
flows, the more intense becomes the action of
the Vital Force, and the more powerful is the
repulsion and expulsion of all dangerous toxins,
morbid matter and waste that are clogging the
cells, tissues, and capillaries. Accordingly, the
general speeding up of the eliminative organs
by the pumping heart and the rushing blood,
is indicative of the greatest cleansing and puri-

fying process of which the living organism is capable. The accompanying symptoms complexes of "disease," such as vomiting, diarrhoea, diphtheria, pneumonia, fevers, smallpox, etc., signify nothing but the various methods adopted by the body for use in purging itself of the dangerous toxins and foreign matter within.

That so-called disease is merely the (4) effects of the body's reaction to dangerous internal elements has been known and understood for ages by a few level-headed, clear-sighted physicians, and is explained in the works of Thomas Sydenham, a master medical man, known as the English Hippocrates. In Vol. 1, p. 29, edition of the Sydenham Society, 1848, we find the following definition of "acute disease" in general:—

"A disease, however much its cause may be adverse to the human body, is nothing more than an effort of Nature, who strains with might and main to restore the health of the patient, by the elimination of the morbific matter."

Three-quarters of a century later Henry Lindlahr, M.D., voiced the same doctrine in these words:—

"Every acute disease is the result of a cleansing and healing effort of Nature (p. 55) . . . All acute diseases are uniform in their causes, their purpose, and, if conditions are favorable, uniform also in their progressive development . . . " (Nature Cure, 20th Edition, 1922).

When the nervous system and the reactive forces become adjusted to the pent-up poisons, there is a state of chronic poisoning, wherein the acute symptoms subside, and some chronic ailment is established, which may be some time in progressing to a distressingly noticeable stage. Or, the organism may be so abused and enervated by "scientific treatment," that a reaction sufficient in power to cast off the poisons, is impossible because of a lack of vitality. Then we also have a chronic condition of some sort, such as Bright's disease, diabetes, cancer, tuberculosis, stomach, liver, or heart trouble, rheumatism, etc. Dr. Lindlahr explains "chronic diseases," as follows:

"To check and suppress acute diseases . . . means to suppress Nature's purifying and healing efforts, to bring about fatal complications, and to change the acute, constructive reactions into chronic disease conditions." (p. 77).

Going back to our man, we observe that he became "diseased" because during his struggle with the enemy, there was a general speeding up of the function of the body for a specific purpose. When the battle began, and cardiac and respiratory action was accelerated, in an earnest effort to supply the additional strength required in the struggle to subdue the foe, suppose that some "scientist," believing that Nature becomes undependable at times, had stopped the fight, at various intervals, long enough to inject into the man's body some drug and serum poisons, that would bring the functions back to normal by stunning the nervous system and retarding the action of all the various organs? Would this help or hinder the man in the struggle? Would it increase or decrease his strength and vitality? Common sense teaches that it would hinder the man and vastly decrease his strength and vitality, for the procedure is contrary to the functions of the body.

In order the better to illustrate our point, we shall say that this is done; for few patients ever pass thru illness without being the subject of such "scientific treatment." The body must continue the struggle, for the internal foe (poison) will not depart of its own accord. It must be thrown out by force. So after the interruption for the first injection of drugs and serums, the battle is resumed, somewhat slowly at first on the part of the body, but with increasing vigor as the body recovers from the stunning effect of the drugs and serums.

The battle is soon in full blast again, with the functions of the body running high, in order to supply the requisite strength to carry on the combat to a successful conclusion. The "scientific treatment" is again administered to slow down the functions. This time the body experiences more difficulty to recover from the

effect than it did the first time. But it gradual-
ly recovers sufficiently to quicken its functions,
in a last desperate attempt to supply the
strength needed to cast out the foe. And once
more is the "scientific treatment" administered
to slow down the functions.

The body, we observe, is struggling against
two enemies: the physician without and his
poisons within, and the original poisons within, which the body endeavored to eliminate by
accelerating its functions. Each time that the
body was making progress in its work, it received a serious shock at the hands of the physician; and each time this shock occurred, it
decreased the body's vitality.

Every living organism is self-operating, self-
adjusting, self-repairing, self-preserving and
self-curing, and so constituted and formed that
each and every function, from birth till death.
tends towards health alone, and never towards
"disease." By virtue of-this, the body will not
only maintain itself in health throughout its
existence, but will even restore itself to normality when any violation of the Law of Life has
created conditions that are incompatible with
its harmonious existence; provided the opportunity be given, and the shock induced by the
destructive agent be not too severe.

The mal-treatment by "science" here illus-,
trated, was continued until the body was so

weakened, that it was at last unable to recover and react because of the gross interference with its functions, and it slowly succumbs,—but not to the power of the enemy, for the enemy it would have readily subdued had it not been hampered in its efforts. But it succumbs to the power of the poisons administered by the "scientific" and misguided physician, who would have the body function as he wants it, and not as Nature would have it.

More harmful and dangerous, and more difficult to eliminate than the different kinds of systemic poisons, originating within the body, are the drugs and serum poisons administered to "cure disease." Every drugless practitioner knows from experience that it is harder to restore a patient who has been under the treatment of an orthodox medical man, and had his body filled with drug and serum poisons, than one who has not been treated. Dr. Ralph M. Crane, an Osteopath of New York, says that during the winter of 1918 he treated 650 cases of flu-pneumonia, and never lost one; and that in the winter of 1922-23 he treated 125 cases of pneumonia and lost not one. He observed:—

"I have never lost one of my own cases, and most of those which come to me after they have been under the care of medical doctors, I can save, with one exception—I cannot do much for patients who have been dosed with morphine, a common practice, I am sorry to say. There is no breaking

through the morphine, even by osteopathy. That
· drug apparently paralyzes every recuperative faculty
a patient possesses."

Knowing that the body is a unit, we know,
that the law which governs the whole, governs
every part. When any part shows signs of sickness, such as throbbing heart, rapid respiration,
rising temperature, and so on (which medical
men term and treat as disease,) we should know
that the whole is affected. More than this, we
should know that the cause of the visible signs
of sickness is merely the (4) secondary effects
of the (3) body's reaction to an (2) internal
danger, the primary cause of which is (1) violation of law; and that the reaction has for its
sole purpose the purging of the body, by its
cleansing forces, of the systemic poisons which
constitute the dangerous element. This being
an abnormal condition, abnormal strength is
required, which can be supplied by abnormal
function alone, and not by drug and serum poisons that are devoid of life and power of action,
and dangerous even to healthy bodies.

Every school boy knows that in running,
jumping, or in performing any strenuous exercise, additional strength must be furnished
for the occasion, and that this is done by the
heart, the lungs, and the other organs, vigor-
ously quickening their normal function. Should
we interfere with this perfect process of Nature,
by slowing down the vital functions with poi-

sons that stun and paralyze the nervous system? Can we safely enforce such an arbitrary law as this upon the living organism, in direct violation of its own constitution?

There is reason and purpose in every function of the body. All its functions are perfect, and are designed to accomplish specific results. These results have for their object the improvement of the organism. To "treat" the affected parts—the parts that exhibit the symptoms of "disease"—is to ignore the purpose of the body to thwart its efforts, and to force upon it an inimical condition that it was striving to cast off. Because we do not understand the body, or its function, or the purpose of its function, does not license any of us, not even "scientists," to assault and attack the body, or any of its parts or functions, with drugs, serums, and knives. To do so must lead only to permanent injury.

We now summarize the cause of disease as follows:—

1—Primary cause: violation of the Law of Life.

2—Primary effect: toxemia-enervation.

3—Secondary cause: the body's reaction to the internal danger.

4—Secondary effect: symptom complexes called disease.

(1) Violation of the Law of Life produces
enervation-toxemia: (2) enervation-toxemia
threatens the body's harmonious existence·
(3) the body reacts to the threatening danger:
and (4) the effect of this reaction is exhibited
at the surface in symptom complexes termed
diseases. of which more than 400 have been
named by diagnostians. To "treat" any "disease" means to "treat" nothing but the effects
of the body's reaction to the dangerous internal
condition that threatens its destruction. and
such course hinders Nature's work.

All substances which, when introduced into
the body, either by cutaneous injection or ab-
sorbtion, by respiration or by ingestion. cannot be utilized as food by the body economy.
are poisonous thereto. Poisons always force the
body to act in self-defense. If the kind and
quantity of poison be insufficient to produce
instant death, it produces death by degrees by
establishing a condition of chronic poisoning
(so-called immunity)—a danger to which the
body adjusts itself only when it cannot control
nor destroy the same. This is observed in the
use of tobacco, when the vital resistance must
first be subdued, by persistence in the practice.
before the body will submit to the poison. In
the finale, the destructive agent, which the body
was unable to control or destroy, and to which
it was forced to yield after its resisting-power
was weakened, will compel the body to destroy
itself by forcing it continually to act in self-

defense, against the ever-present danger, until its Vital Force is exhausted, resulting in a collapse of the nervous system that ultimately brings death.

Every rational person knows that exhaustion kills, even though the body be, in every particular, healthy and vigorous. Twenty-five centuries ago, when the Greeks won the great victory of Marathon, the messenger who brought the news to Athens, ran the entire distance on foot, more than 26 miles, and fell dead from exhaustion as he delivered his message. The machinery of the body functioned so violently and so long, to meet the extraordinary demand made on it, that it simply collapsed from the exhaustive strain.

Diabetes mellitus is a chronically poisoned state of the body, in which the most marked symptom is an excessive amount of saccharine matter and albumin in the urine: All cases of diabetes are benefitted by nothing more than an absolute fast of several days. A diet of uncooked fruits, greens, and vegetables, following the fast, often "cures" the most malignant cases Why do we suggest "uncooked" food? Because no animal, save man, attempts to subsist on "cooked" food; and God has made no exception to law in favor of man in food preparation or in any other particular. Consequently, here is the (1) primary cause (violation of law) responsible for the chronic poisoning, of which diabetes is one of the many (4) secondary ef-fects. The self-curative power of the body cor-rects the effect when a chance is given by a re-moval of the cause; but the effect will return if the cause is resumed.

The (1) primary cause (violation of law) of diabetes is without the body, and is known only by its effect (diabetes) within. Medical men search within for the cause, discover the effect, call that the cause, and Fred Banting "discovers" insulin to "cure" the effect, mistak-en for cause, while the cause (violation of law) unnoticed and untouched, remains to continue its deadly work, regardless of all "medical cures"; and Dr. Banting is hailed as the "med-ical wizard" of the age, and showered with dignities and riches.

In due time, the cause sends the sufferer to an early grave, and weeping friends are evasively told that they waited too long before seeking the services of a "specialist." A profession that forever fails, yet is able by plausible excuse to conceal the cause of its failure, can persuade the gullible public into believing that it is a success, by skillfully shifting the responsibility for its failure to the shoulders of the credulous ones whom it serves and deceives. It requires super-education to enable a deceiver to mis-represent facts so cunningly as to exonerate himself in the eyes of his trusted patients and patrons. "The serpent was more subtile than any beast of the field which God had made."

As surely as every word must go back to the alphabet for its letter-element, just as surely must every "disease" go back to a violation of the Law of Life for its primary cause. And since the secondary cause of "disease" comes from the body's reaction to the dangerous internal condition, we know that every "acute disease" is nothing more or less than the effect of a vigorous effort of the body to protect itself against injurious agents. In other words, that it is purely a curative process in itself, being the normal reaction of the living organism to its environment, and conducted under the guidance of an Infinite Wisdom and Power, that can tolerate no interference from human hands, even though offered in a spirit of helpfulness. These vital facts, for fact they are, cannot be reiterated too frequently, nor urged too strongly.

Another point that cannot be too often repeated is this: The signs and symptoms manifested by the body in so-called disease, are not due to the action of the internal poison, in an effort to destroy the organism; for dead matter, being devoid of life, is ipso facto devoid of any power of action. These symptoms, as we have said, are purely the secondary effects of the body's reaction to the internal danger; and when we "treat disease," we simply counteract and suppress the outward signs of the body's efforts to protect itself. There being no such thing as "disease," there can be nothing to treat; and when we do "treat disease," all we accomplish is the counteraction and suppression of the body's natural action of self-protection.

The same is true of all so-called remedies. Drugs and serums do not and cannot act on the body. They are dead matter, and dead matter is powerless to act. As Dr. Walter observes:—

". . . If drugs are the real cause,—that is, if they communicate the power which performs vital functions and produces vital vigor,—there will be 'invariable connection' between the drug and the function. There will be no function without the drug; and there will be an increase or decrease of function corresponding to any increase or decrease of the drug. The absurdity of such a claim is evident; it rests only on superstition by indifference . . ." (Vital Science, p. 263).

It is the body that acts, and not the drug, serum or body waste. It is the danger inherent in the poisonous nature of these things that prompts the body to act. The action is in self-defense, and is produced by a calling out of the body's reserve forces; just as the danger of the enemy prompted the man to act in self-defense, and struggle until his strength was exhausted. The effects of the abnormal action is beating heart, throbbing brain, rapid respiration, profuse perspiration, vomiting, diarrhoea, skin eruptions, fevers, etc. The nature and locality of the symptoms is what determines the name the physicians give them, and that is incidental and immaterial. The more poisonous any substance is, the more dangerous it is, and the quicker and harder the body acts—sending a large dose of salts or castor oil thru the alimentary canal with a rush. Such treatment, instead of its being curative, is destructive; for it is a terrible shock to the nervous system, and may be continued until the body will utterly collapse from the exhaustion induced by its own violent efforts, of self-protection.

From what has been said and shown, we observe how clear it is that the first and only step to be taken in the prevention and "cure" of any "disease," is to obey the Law. But the thought that obeying the Law of Life redounds to one's greatest good now and forever, seems never to have entered into man's philosophy. The Law of Life is the Law of the Universe; the Law of the Universe is the Law of God. The road to an understanding of God and His work, is from the seed to the plant, and from the plant to the seed again.

We repeat: Here is the profound principle from which Great Nature operates. Medical science (?) has made many "discoveries," but

here is one that has been overlooked, in spite
of all the brilliant workers, their super-education, their vast expenditures of money, their
endless research work, experiments, sacrifice of
life, and so on. At the Center is Simplicity and
Unity of cause (the Life Principle), while at
the Surface is Infinite Variety of Appearance
of sickness, exhibited in the various and mystifying symptom complexes of disease, termed
mumps, measles, catarrh, eczema, pneumonia,
typhoid, smallpox, cancer, and so on, which
infinite Variety of Appearance "scientists" have
been studying, naming, and treating for thirty
centuries, and to which they have attached the
highest importance, while the Simplicity and
Unity of Cause at the Center remains neglected,
unknown, and obscure.

Medical science (?) has never studied nor
investigated anything pertaining to "disease,"
except the Infinite Variety of Appearance at
the Surface, which they have done to the total
exclusion of all else. These they study, name
and treat, while the Simplicity and Unity of
Cause at the Center is entirely ignored and utt-
terly disregarded. For thirty centuries they have
thought entirely from the eye (appearance),
and this has blinded their understanding and
closed up their will; and from a freedom that
is in accord with its reason, the will does only
that which has been confirmed in the understanding. The understanding is blinded not
only by ignorance, but equally by false doctrine.

For as Truths open the understanding, so Falsities close it up.

It follows from what has been said and shown, that sickness comes from within, not from without. Sickness indicates the effect of the Life Principle within, actively engaged in trying to save the body from destruction. The kind of sickness—the surface symptoms—while resulting from the Unity of Cause at the Center, may be and is as variable at the surface, as to medical diagnosis, as are the winds of the earth, or the products of the soil. We may diagnose these symptoms—variety of Appearance at the Surface—as mumps, measles, catarrh, consumption, cancer, smallpox, etc., as we similarly name the various products of the soil as wheat, corn, oats, many kinds of grasses, weeds, trees, etc.; but regardless of the arbitrary names of the symptoms at the suface, they all come from the center in one cause!

When we know the principles from which Nature operates, and realize that ALL illness comes from Unity of Cause at the Center (poisoned blood), regardless of the medical names of the infinite Variety of Appearance at the Surface, we then understand how futile it is to search for symptoms (symptomatology), how fruitless it is to name these symptoms (diagnosis), and how useless it is to treat and suppress these symptoms (therapeutics). Useless did we say?   Destructive is a far better and more fitting term.

The healer who knows the principles from which Nature operates, puts no dependence in such changeable and unreliable signs as symptoms, and cares less for their medical names. He directs his attention not to these, since they have to do only with effects, and not with the Unity of Cause at the Center.   Cause is one thing and effect is another. The difference between the two is similar to the difference between prior and subsequent, or between that which forms and that which is formed. Effects may be studied to eternity, but such process will not reveal the cause.   That is why all medical practice books state that—

"the cause of disease is unknown;"

and why Dr. Osler, America's greatest physician, declared:

"of (the cause of) disease we know nothing at all."

God is cause and man is effect. We may study man (effect) to eternity, and yet know nothing regarding God (cause). Every effect is visible, while every cause is invisible, and can be discovered, not by studying effects, but—

Only by keeping the understanding for a long time in spiritual light.

When we study effects, we think from the eye; in the study of cause we must necessarily think from the understanding, since causes are invisible. But medical men study effects, and think from the eye, and of such people Swedenborg observes:—

They think from the eye, and are not able to think from the understanding. Thought from the eye closes the understanding, but thought from understanding opens the eye.

Accordingly, the healer who thinks from the understanding (cause at the center), and not from the eye (appearance at the surface), understands the principles from which Nature operates, and directs his efforts to the Unity of Cause at the Center (blood), and not to the Variety of Appearance at the Surface (symptoms). When the Unity of Cause at the Center (blood) grown normal, because of right living, and never because of any treatment, medical or otherwise, the Infinite Variety of Appearance at the Surface will wither and die, as the plants in a field after their roots have been cut in sunder. These plants may be wheat, corn, oats, grass, or trees; but when their roots have been severed, they wither and die, regardless of their names. The surface symptoms of illness may be diagnosed as mumps, measles, catarrh, cancer, smallpox, and so on, but they cannot live and thrive when the blood has been clarified and purified. They must wither, die, and disappear.

The whole matter may be properly summar-
ized as follows:——

1—Life is the creative force, functioning in
the body. In health it functions smoothly and
silently. When its function is obstructed, it
struggles to save the body by conquering the
obstructing object or condition. This struggle
is termed diseased, and named according to lo-
cation of symptoms. There is no such. thing
as disease per se.

2—The continuous and harmonious existence of the body depends upon strict compli-
ance with the Law of Life written in every part
and particle of its structure.

3—The body is created complete and perfect, wanting in nothing, and incapable of re-
ceiving anything from human hands. It is
self-operating, self-regulating, self-repairing,
self-preserving, and self-curing.

4—All the healing power in the Universe is
within the body.

5—No power, force, substance, or thing is
able to. save the body or serve the healing
power within, further than to remove the ob-
struction responsible for its disturbed equilibrium.

6—The life of the flesh is in the blood. The life of all flesh is the blood thereof. (Lev. 17:11,14).

7—Insofar as the blood remains active and normal, and to that degree only, will and must all organs, tissues, and cells remain healthy and normal.

8—In ·direct ratio as the blood becomes stagnant, foul, impure, and abnormal, will and must all organs, tissues, and cells show a decline from the normal. This is disease.

The life of all flesh is the blood thereof, and as the condition of the blood is, so must the condition of the flesh be. For as the continuous existence of the body is dependent wholly upon the blood, it must follow that good health or poor health depends upon and springs from the blood. So the vital stream that turns the wheels of life is not only the health-producing and life-sustaining power but also the disease-producing power. It could not be otherwise without reversing law and order. Therefore, the healer who knows the principles from which Nature operates, takes the following position:—

1—The continuous existence of the body depends upon the blood.

2—A normal flow of normal blood brings health.

3—Retarded circulation and foul, impure blood brings disease.

4—Purification of the blood and acceleration of the circulation is scientific treatment. There can be no other.

5—The means to accomplish this are supplied by the body alone. The body makes blood and purifies it. Nothing else can do this work.

6—The supply determines the method of procedure.

7—The procedure must be natural; and, being natural, results are and must be favorable and permanent.

Everything in the Universe is governed by Law. If we know the law and apply it, there invariably follows results so certain as to be amazing because of their positiveness. We can prevision and predict, with prefect accuracy, the results of certain actions and conditions. This is the Law of Cause and Effect. Man has applied this Law with startling success to many things, but seems never to have considered applying it to his own body. Does man, in his pride and vanity, believe that he is so far apart from Nature, that Nature's laws apply not to him? Is he too proud to acknowledge obedience to his Master? The proper application of God's Law is merely obedience to His command; and by strictly obeying the Law, man eliminates all uncertainty as to disease, just as he, in the same way, eliminates all uncertainty as to all other things; and Health then flows as silently, freely, and naturally, as the tide rises and falls. Why not? They are all governed by the same Law!

WE WOULD LIKE TO HEAR FROM YOU

We would like to know if this book has been profitable to the reader. If anything in it has given you pleasure and happiness, if you have received knowledge and benefits from it.

Please write it down and let us know about it. Even if you only send a post card with your name and address and a few remarks—it will be greatly appreciated.

NATURAL SCIENCE SOCIETY

IMPORTANT

You can obtain information, freely and without obligation, concerning courses, books, literature, etc., by Kenyon Klamonti by sending in your request.

Write to **NATURAL SCIENCE SOCIETY**
2803 S. Bumby Street
ORLANDO, FLORIDA

BUILD HEALTH . . . . . REGENERATE YOURSELF

YOU HAVE THE POWER WITHIN

You have all the necessary power, potentialities within your body to build and maintain health.

You may get temporary relief thru therapeutic treatment, but such treatment only stimulates or excites, inhibits or suppresses the reparatory powers in the body.

The only way to build health is the NATURAL WAY which means living in obedience to the Laws of Life, Nature and Health. Efforts to find any other way will forever end in failure.

The vital factors that compose the nature requirements of Good Health are—air, water, food, sunshine, exercise, sleep and relaxation, mind, sex conservation, temperature, climate.

There is good health and bad health, but no disease. The symptoms of bad health the doctors are trained to study, group together and give names and are all put under the one heading of disease, which they say must be "cured."

But no treatments are necessary, no remedies are required, no cures needed. Follow the principles of health and you will build good health. Bad health will go just as night disappears when day dawns . . . when there is light—darkness is gone.

By correcting your habits and by living in a healthful environment, bad health will disappear — without any therapeutic treatment. Stop impairing your health by wasting your vitality in bad habits and in artificial conditions.

Our early Ancestors survived thru the Ages without present day therapeutic treatments. Plants, birds and animals of nature survive without the aid of medical art. It is natural for you to have good health—it is your birthright.

If you follow destructive and unnatural habits, and the artificial life of so called civilization, you can expect degeneration, decreased vitality and bad health.

People are forever searching for some "wonder cure." They go from one therapeutic treatment to another. Their search will be endless. Why look without when the power is within the body—waiting for the chance to prove its presence, if only given an opportunity.

Health is natural; get back to Nature and live the Healthful Life. Why worry about symptoms—effects. Remove the cause and the symptoms will disappear. Follow the natural way of living—in harmony with the Laws of Life, Nature and Health and you will have good health; you will radiate a natural beauty of color, your skin will have a fine texture, you will have vim, vigor and vitality; you will have good posture, form, expression and animation.

HAPPINESS . . . comes from HEALTH.
HEALTH . . . Comes from RIGHT LIVING.
RIGHT LIVING means obedience to the LAW of LIFE.

Do *YOU* know that LAW???
We teach it . . .

LIFTED 1,006,000 POUNDS in 34 MINUTES and 35 SECONDS AFTER EATING NOTHING FOR THREE WEEKS

A mystery, so far unsolved by science, is the SOURCE of Man's strength, energy and vitality. Biologists say they come from food, but overwhelming evidence shows this theory is wrong

GILMAN LOWE, weight lifter and health director, after FASTING for three weeks, mounted a scale adjusted to 1,000 pounds net The scale was equipped with a steel platform, against which Lowe braced his back. He braced and lifted 1,006 times in succession, until the scale each time registered half a ton—a total of 1,006,000 pounds in 34 minutes and 35 seconds.

Lowe did that after **EATING NOTHING FOR THREE WEEKS.** This test of strength and endurance shows that man's strength and vitality does not depend on food but on something else—Do YOU know what?

GET a copy of **BREATH AND BLOOD** by Kenyon Klamonti. It will help you to understand HEALTH and problems which have previously confused you—it will bring you into a NEW REALIZATION and answer questions such as—

Do you know the function that is the secret of living and the three things necessary to maintain and sustain the body?

Do you know the primary purpose of eating and drinking is NOT to supply the blood with nourishment for the body? Colds and deep seated aches and pains (rheumatism) have one chief cause—do you know what it is?

Do you know what is meant by Breath of Death—which cannot be detected by our five senses and can kill quicker than the venom of a rattler?

One thousand people died in two minutes in World War II —do you know the cause?

Do you know why many patients develop pneumonia in hospitals—especially after operations?

A sneeze, cough, cold, headache is a warning to you—do you know what the warning is?

EXTRACTS FROM A FEW OF THE MANY ENTHUSIASTIC LETTERS FROM READERS.

Vista, CALIFORNIA

"Please permit me to offer my profound thanks to the author of the books which I have just read THRICE, to wit BREATH AND BLOOD, THE NUTRITIONAL MYTH, HEALTH SCIENCE and SCIENTIFIC LIVING

"These books have forced me to revise, somewhat reluctantly, of course, a good many of my former 'College degree' ideas about the whole subject of Health This I am glad to do because now, for the first time I have a clear picture framed in my mind of both the 'beginning and the end',—as it were of what it means to attempt true healing in patients I would insistently recommend these books to everyone interested in knowing the true facts, especially those whose mission it is to help an ailing Humanity "

Dr. Amil H Sprehn,
Member International Society
of Naturopathic Physicians

Bicknell, INDIANA

"I have been reading SCIENTIFIC LIVING and find it a wonderful revelation. I have also read HEALTH SCIENCE which is also wonderful and full of truths "

"C R "

Indian Orchard, MASS

"The more I read of your works the more my eyes open up "

"Mrs G J "

Hartford, CONN

"I have read your lessons on SCIENTIFIC LIVING and HEALTH SCIENCE and find in them the pearl of great price or the needle which was lost in a hay stack

"If people were to sow these seed truths contained in your writings then humanity would know the kingdom of God on earth

"I have passed my 71st birthday and have studied many courses and researched in comparative religions but I have never found anything so analytical as your course IMMORTALISM. May God bless your Society and all who partake of its knowledge

"Let me know as soon as 'LONGEVITY' is ready "

"Dr Monroe E Ruth"

Why is it we are able to drag out a miserable existence of
50-60 years in an environment which would quickly kill a
vigorous, healthy, wild Indian?

What is meant by "immunity" and what expense to the
vital functions is involved?

For the ANSWERS to these questions and other VALU-
ABLE and STARTLING information, obtainable from no
other source, which is of the utmost IMPORTANCE to
YOU—Send $1.00 for your copy which will be sent IM-
MEDIATELY.

THE NUTRITIONAL MYTH

The famous Dr. Carrel in his book—MAN, THE UN-
KNOWN, says the body is not made of extraneous material (food and drink). It is composed of cells that come
from the Parent Cell.

The Parent Cell is NOT the product of food, nor is it sustained by food. What food does not and cannot produce,
it cannot and does not sustain.

Dr. Carrel goes on to say, "Our ignorance (of the body s
constitution and function) is profound."

GET a copy of **THE NUTRITIONAL MYTH** by Kenyon
Klamonti. It will really get you thinking along new lines
—you may not believe the title—THE NUTRITIONAL
MYTH—but investigate, you will be AMAZED, and finish
by scratching your head and asking, "Why should man
eat?"

Do you know the billions of cells forming the body are said
to be suns and stars, composed of the same cosmic substance and governed by the same cosmic LAW? Do YOU
know what that substance is?

There are six primary steps on the path to REGENERA-
TION; do YOU know them?

Do you believe the modern theory of nourishment is a
myth?

If you would like the answer to these questions and to
read this new work—which so many people are reading
and talking about send in $1.00 to the publishers of this
book TODAY

Miami, FLORIDA

"Enjoy the lessons very much and am enlightened on many subjects which previously I had only a slight knowledge. Keep up the good work. Am enclosing names of persons who I believe will be interested."

"H. C. F."

Baltimore, MARYLAND

"Have read your excellent works—BREATH AND BLOOD, THE NUTRITIONAL MYTH, HEALTH SCIENCE, SCIENTIFIC LIVING and the course IMMORTAL-. ISM.

"What priceless knowledge—I can sincerely recommend them to anyone interested in building good health and living a fuller life.

"What a tremendous amount of research must have been necessary to compile the material for his teachings are so revolutionary yet the truth and fully in accord with the Laws of Nature.

"All should read these inspiring works "

"Mrs. F. B."

Cedar Brook, NEW JERSEY

"Have been very much interested in THE NUTRITIONAL MYTH. It is a wonderful book, every human being should read it Enclosed is check for your two books—HEALTH SCIENCE and SCIENTIFIC LIVING.

"May God bless and keep you."

"M. A. C."

Los Angeles, CALIFORNIA

"Many thousands of persons are in need of your wonderful 'God Science teachings' due to the wide spread confusion in Nutrition circles plus the erroneous information put forward by the so-called Dietetic experts.

"These works, for me at least, have been the climax of over 30 years study and research in the related fields of the 'All Best Methods,' etc. I look forward to more of your works."

"C. T. D."

Detroit, MICHIGAN

"In your publications I was pleased to find the information and knowledge for which I have searched all my life."

"P. N "

HE LIVED 370 YEARS.
GREW FOUR NEW SETS OF TEETH AND HAIR
TURNED FROM BLACK TO GREY FOUR TIMES

In his "Believe It Or Not," Ripley stated: "Numas De Cugna of Bengal, India, lived to be 370 years old. He grew FOUR new sets of teeth, and his hair turned from black to grey FOUR times He died in 1566."

Do YOU believe this? Ripley claimed all his findings were true

You think the DARK AGES are gone because you are asleep AWAKE! Your boasted liberty and enlightenment are largely imaginary. You cannot miss what you never had

ALEXIS CARREL, one of the GREATEST physicians of modern times wrote:

"In fact, our ignorance (of the body and its functions) is profound " - MAN, THE UNKNOWN, p. 4

History shows that people who LIVE LONGEST have little or NOTHING to do with doctors, putting their TRUST IN NATURE. By turning to Nature after given up as HOPELESS by the doctors, LUDOVICO CORNARO, GODDARD DIAMOND, and JOHN BAILES recovered HEALTH and lived 103, 120 and 128 years respectively

But reliable literature teaching people HOW to let NATURE GUIDE them is hard to get because of being suppressed and distorted by the doctors to protect their business

After years of research we have found what we regard as the best works on this subject and offer them to those who would enjoy HEALTH as GOD intends for ALL to have. The works are as follows:

HEALTH SCIENCE	SCIENTIFIC LIVING
Eternal Physical Life.	Recuperation.
Life and Time	Rejuvenation.
Fountain of Youth.	Longevity (A).
Physiological Time.	Longevity (B).
The Perfect Machine.	Longevity (C).
Pathological Age.	Life (A).
Decrepitude	Life (B).

Price of EACH post-paid $1.00

Send for all four—BREATH AND BLOOD, THE NUTRITIONAL MYTH, HEALTH SCIENCE and SCIENTIFIC LIVING   Only $3 50.